Unlocking systemic wisdom

Bringing key knowledge from constellations to the work floor

Unlocking systemic wisdom – *Bringing key knowledge from constellations to the work floor*

Siets Bakker & Leanne Steeghs

Photography: Espérance Blaauw

Translation by: Joscelyn Weychan, Bonnie McClellan-Broussard

Originally published under title: Systemisch Wijzer, Uitgeverij Thema, Zaltbommel, 2015

© 2017 (v4), Het Noorderlicht

ISBN 978-9492331717 (NUR 470)

Inhoudsopgave

Foreword

"Would you like her to stand next to you?", the therapist asked, and to give force to his words he moved the piece of paper that represented "her" a little closer. A warm feeling passed through my stomach. Yes, someone next to me, I liked that. In spite of the fact that I had been in a relationship for years, I knew what to do.

I could have hesitated for months and tried to reach a decent, rational decision through conversation, but secretly my body already knew the answer. Even though I, as a philosopher, have a rational mind, I dared to listen to my body. Fortunately so. That body and meaning are interwoven becomes clear from such words as "supressing", "embracing" and "not looking forward to something". These are physical terms that also have (been given) an abstract meaning. It is actually quite logical that my body "knows" profound, essential information about me; it is more surprising that my body seems capable of passing on that information to other bodies. I can tell others how I feel and what I am thinking about. I then use words in the hope that my thoughts and feelings are interpreted correctly by the other. However, I can also tell my story by holding on to the other, making him sit somewhere, lifting him up or pushing him away. It is amazing to experience how much you can convey this way and how much you can learn about yourself and others by doing so. I have no idea how it works exactly. I am averse to woolliness, and as scientific as a philosopher can be; however, I am sure that it works and I would love for everybody to experience it for themselves at least once.

Bas Haring
philosopher, writer of popular science literature and professor

The experience described by Bas is exactly the experience many people have when they come into contact with systemic work through a constellation, as did we. We wondered how this wisdom could be used and applied in everyday life. For example, in your work, close to your own experience. That is what this book is about.

Siets Bakker and Leanne Steeghs

Introduction

IN A workshop with a group of HR advisers I asked what the most important competence was in their daily work. 'Persuading' was mentioned most often. Every time that someone gave this answer, my stomach clenched. I realised how tough the work of an HR advisor in this organisation must be if you spent all day persuading other people. My own body remembered how I had once worked in a similar setting, constantly in search of 'the best option'. Working from my systemic wisdom has made my life a great deal lighter. No longer do I always have to persuade people. I can increasingly work from the larger whole, without judging. I can simply follow the movement. The struggle is becoming less and less.

AT THE postgraduate training institute for coaches I meet lots of enthusiastic participants who are extremely eager to learn. It sometimes happens that I'm not able to answer their questions straight away. In the beginning, when I had just started working there, I struggled with not being able to know everything; it made me feel slightly embarrassed, especially here, as a teacher at this level. The result was that I did my utmost to find a fitting answer or perform a smart intervention, but that only caused me to get more stuck in my head. Now that I have better access to my systemic wisdom I have increasingly fewer issues with staying in the area of 'not knowing'. I can now deal with the uncomfortable feeling that accompanies this. In the meantime the deep trust I've developed together with countless experiences have shown me that an answer or a direction will always emerge.

We coined the term "systemic wisdom" from the philosophy of systemic work together with family and organisational constellations. We translated this philosophy into an everyday practicable form. This ensures that after you read this book you will not only have gained knowledge, but that you can actually benefit from it in your everyday work and life.

Rarely do you have to accept the words or the terminology used as an absolute truth. We describe systemic concepts, principles and uses from our own knowledge. We do not follow the principles of a single training institute or movement. We have consciously used varied terms and terminology in order to acknowledge everything. These terms can be similar and sometimes they emphasise a slightly different aspect. Choosing a single word or term would detract from the space and depth of systemic work.

Systemic wisdom is certainly not something that has to be developed or created. It is already there. In you as an individual, but also in the groups, teams, and organisations you are a part of. It is an enormous source of information that we all could use much more often, also in our culture and education.

By "turning on" your own systemic wisdom, you can tap into an entirely new source of information. Without having to work very hard, you will be able to connect to a larger whole and access a deeper level of "knowing". The gateway to your systemic wisdom is your own body. We have become so accustomed to acquiring knowledge through our brains that our systemic wisdom is often less (consciously) developed. Becoming systemically wiser is learning to feel, to trust and daring to act on the signals made available by your surroundings and by your body. Reading a book about it is an excellent start!

In this book we share our insights and experiences with the intention to stimulate you as a reader to make more use of your own systemic wisdom. Our experience has taught us that your entire consciousness increases when you learn to trust your systemic observations. This helps you recognise what is truly going on in a situation more quickly. You will also notice an increased sharpness in your observations and an improved sensitivity for nuances. This clarity will make it easier to rely on your "internal compass" in your life and work, simply because it will become easier to trust your sense of what feels right and what does not. Your reach will widen and you will receive more opportunities, without even having to try very hard!

You will read how to incorporate systemic work into your own life, as an individual and as a professional. This does not mean that non-systemic work is wrong or, even worse, no longer advisable. We are of the opinion that adding possibilities to your current resources is always positive. This book is definitely not a plea to start approaching everything in a systemic way from now on. Throughout the whole book you will find examples and exercises in which we share our own experiences. This shows that developing your systemic wisdom is simple and accessible to anyone. In the final chapter we have included several methods to enable you to experiment and practice with the material you have read and learnt.

Avoid working too hard whilst reading this book. There is no need to retain or record anything. Some theoretical knowledge is required, but it will not make the difference. Allow yourself to go with the flow during reading. You will automatically notice what grabs your attention and what "sticks".

Trust that you will pick up on what you currently need most. That is enough. If you read the book again in a few years' time, you might pick up on entirely different things.

Siets Bakker and Leanne Steeghs

1 The World of Systems

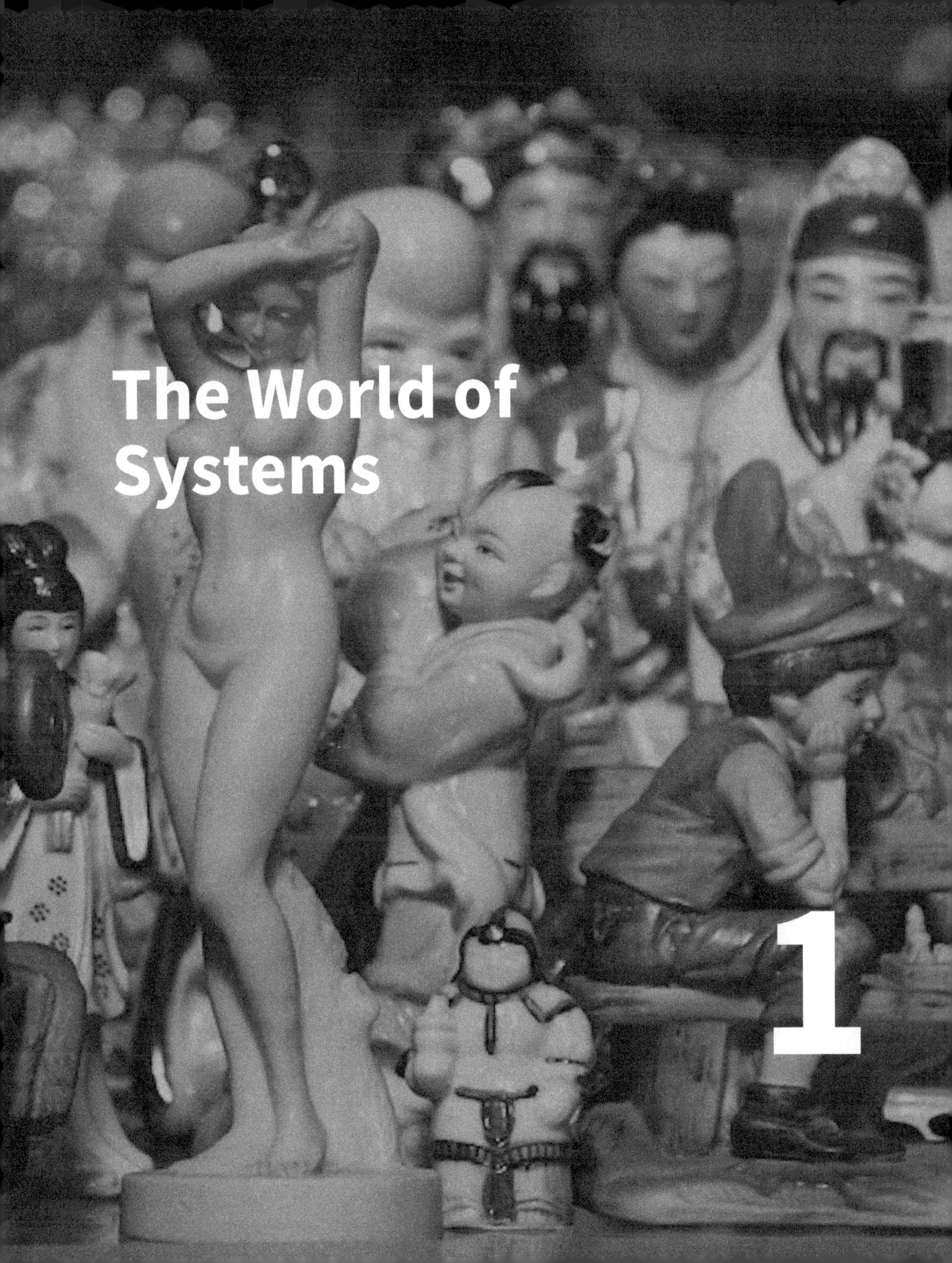

1.1 What "systemic" means

"Systemic" is something of a strange word in English. It is a German concept that is difficult to translate. The term was introduced by Gunthard Weber, one of the first people to do constellations within organisations. It translates roughly as "relating to a whole system". Even though systemic is not originally an English word, the concept has been fully accepted. Systemic is by no means a corruption of the word "systematic".

In our education and daily work we mainly use our analytical skills. In short, the term analytical implies thinking in terms of direct cause and effect. The systemic approach is phenomenological instead of analytical.

Phenomenological means studying situations in their original context: you allow the phenomena to speak for themselves, without wanting to add or change something. Instead of breaking the system down into separate parts, you look at the larger whole. You constantly question which larger whole causes the current situation or problem.

In systemic logic you assume that reality has multiple layers. This layered structure is present always and everywhere. We call the explicitly visible layers at the surface the "overcurrent". The overcurrent can be observed through the symptoms at the surface. Symptoms can take the form of problems or certain (unwanted) behaviour. In organisations, these are the symptoms that call for intervention. However, there are also pleasant or desired symptoms, such as flow, fun and innovation. Strangely enough, these symptoms are hardly ever a reason to start an investigation. We only start researching once something goes wrong or an unwanted situation arises. Initially, we intervene in the overcurrent. These interventions at symptom level usually concern the contents or the procedures. Sometimes this is sufficient to solve a problem or achieve a change in behaviour.

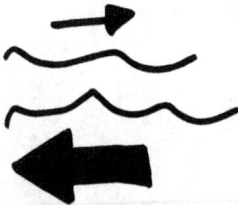

Mariska is a receptionist. She has the habit of arriving at work ten minutes late every day. After a while it starts to annoy her colleagues. They have to cover for her if the telephone rings early in the morning. What annoys them in particular is that Mariska takes it for granted that they will answer the phone for her. When the team manager addresses the issue he finds out that Mariska is always late, not just to work. She experiences

---

difficulty in managing her time. They agree that she will attend a time management course. If she is late more than three times in the coming year, her contract will be terminated. Mariska got the message, took the necessary steps and did not arrive late again.

Unfortunately, reality is often more complicated. An intervention in the overcurrent does not always have the desired effect. If that is the case, symptoms often recur. Problems arise again. Or people, teams and organisations relapse into old habits once the pressure of the intervention disappears. In such cases of "repetitive patterns" it can pay off to investigate the undercurrent. Instead of only tackling the symptoms, you look into the roots of the problem or the behaviour. Interventions in the undercurrent often concern interactions or feelings that are present, but are not discussed because they are taboo, or only latently or subconsciously present. From twenty years of experience with systemic work and constellations, three life-giving forces have been formulated that apply to each system: belonging, order and exchange. These three life-giving forces in the undercurrent of all systems are universal and timeless. That also makes them older than systemic work itself! Being aware of the life-giving forces feels like having an extra sensor, enabling you to intervene more effectively and efficiently than before.

Peter is a mechanic. He often arrives late at work. His colleagues complain about him because productive working time is lost and their entire schedule gets mixed up. The team manager addresses this issue and looks into the problem. Before the reorganisation – five years ago – Peter was never late. The team manager notices how Peter starts to light up when he talks about the past. Peter still feels that something was taken from him and that he has received nothing in return. The team manager says he can imagine that this affects Peter. A deep sigh follows. Peter realises how important it is to feel acknowledged. He seems relieved and says: "*Well, life goes on.*" With these words Peter closes a chapter. Together they "*negotiate*" about the new balance: what are the possibilities and what is expected of Peter? Ever since Peter has arrived on time. He offers plenty of ideas during work meetings and is actively involved with the team.

Symptoms in the overcurrent – such as problems or certain behaviour – can act as a signal for what is happening in the undercurrent. The symptom points out to the system that there is a disturbance (one or more) in the life-giving forces in the undercurrent. Becoming systemically wiser is also about developing a language for these life-giving forces so that you can express what you always sensed.

It is up to you how you approach a situation. The way you define a problem determines which solutions are possible. We tend to zoom in on a problem and then think of a solution. It can be sufficient to tackle symptoms in this way. However, if a problem is recurrent or shows up in several areas, it can be worthwhile to look at it in a systemic way. From a systemic perspective you can define a problem as a part of a larger system. You assume that incidents rarely have a straightforward cause-effect relationship. On the contrary: sometimes very persistent patterns underlie them, possibly beyond the conscious awareness of the people involved. If you work at a systemic level you also work with the mutual relationships and the energy of that system. You realise that you will see roughly the same patterns in the larger system if you look at an incident from a distance. Think of it as a hologram: each part contains the features of the whole.

" Instead of zooming in on a problem,

you zoom out to see the bigger picture. "

It is the opposite of what we are told in today's era of individualism, in which you as an individual have full control over your fate. You can do everything, as long as you really want to and your achievements can only be attributed to yourself. Systemically you could say that every person – but also a product, concept or organisation – is connected by intangible strings. Connected to other systems, to long forgotten events and intentions. Acknowledging the existence of these connections asks for a different, less individual approach. Instead of zooming in on a problem or person, you zoom out when looking at a situation in a systemic way. For example, what can you see when you zoom out from the issue around self-employed people? Maybe you are self-employed yourself and you might feel that it is a completely individual and personal choice. From a systemic perspective you might wonder what solution self-employment provides and why so many people choose self-employment.

" *Work with the whole to influence the parts.* "

People generally think in a linear or circular way. Linear thinking is thinking in terms of cause and effect. Circular thinking zooms in on repetitive patterns, in which the one is the logical consequence of the other. In a systemic approach, you do not use either linear or circular thinking. You approach what you see, hear, feel and think as a whole. Everything that is possible, exists simultaneously. The past is now. The future is now. This is how events from the past still affect our daily lives, especially when people or organisations pretend they never existed.

My nine-year-old son has a school subject called "news awareness". It's a mix between history and biology with a link to current events. Every now and then, the children receive an information sheet to take home and learn by heart. One day he came home with a sheet about "time". The sheet stated that time was linear. There is a past, a present and a future. Everything that exists today finds its roots in the past. He also learnt that there are seasons that follow each other. Like a circle, with a fixed order. A never-ending cycle, without a beginning and without an end. In the phenomenological approach, that includes systemic wisdom, time does not play a role. Everything exists simultaneously.

SB

Traumatic or negative experiences are stored in the system and affect the present and the future. They are passed on through generations, without people even being aware of this. The same goes for positive experiences. However, these do not affect us negatively and are thus less visible in the present. These positive experiences from the past can be strong sources in the here and now. Systemically speaking, a person's behaviour is not a single person's behaviour but rather an indication of what is happening on a systemic level. It is as if that person is "employed" by the greater whole to do or represent something, without being conscious of it.

LS My parents both come from large catholic farming families with lots of children. Every penny was counted, especially in my mother's family. The land and the cattle owned by my mother's family were barely enough to feed eleven children. Nothing was wasted, old clothing was mended and burnt potatoes were eaten too. My brother and I had a very different childhood. Our fridge was always full. When there was a reason to celebrate there was always plenty of cake. Even so my parents did teach me to be economical. In my own way I pass that on to my own children. For example, I come up with meals prepared with yesterday's leftovers, so nothing goes to waste. I might seem economical and I am sure that my children are also economical, in their own way. Not because it is part of my or their nature, but because we are part of a system in which being economical was of vital importance.

The systemic approach is fundamentally different from the linear and circular approaches. Systemically seen, everything exists at the same time and everything is possible. What you see depends on what you zoom in on and from which perspective you look. Just like in a kaleidoscope or a hologram, every part of the system – whether it is an organisation, a team or a family – consists of the properties of the whole.

" *Everything that is possible exists simultaneously.* "

In general, a team or a department acts the same way as the organisation does. The manifestations are different but essentially the patterns are the same. The effects of the behaviour are also different, because the reach of a team is smaller than that of a whole organisation. You can see individual team members demonstrate the same characteristics as the organisation. An organisation often subconsciously selects its employees by these characteristics, giving them priority over knowledge and experience: *"Does this person suit us? Does this person match our attitude, behaviours and 'mores'?"* The system you are dealing with shows the same pattern every time, only on a different scale.

My customer base consists largely of organisations that function well at an operational level. Directors and employees are always busy with what has to happen now and like to tackle problems; an industrious ad hoc culture with plenty of "forward" energy. I can tell by the fast pace ("hurry up") and the action orientation (*"go get 'em"*) during conversations with the management. They want me to provide a training that is as short, quick and practical as possible. They have come to the right person, because I love tackling problems and I do have a lot of "forward" energy. The system energy of these organisations suits me and it is tempting to go along with it. However, if I would do exactly what they asked, the result would be "more of the same". The true growth potential of these organisations can be realised when attention is paid to other or undiscovered qualities, like learning to slow down and reflect, paying attention to the past, and taking a long-term view. Naturally this approach should be balanced out with action and decisiveness, otherwise it lacks connection with the core qualities of the organisation.

LS

1.2 Systems of all types and sizes

You are part of many different systems. Sometimes you choose to belong to a system, like a sports club, your social circle, a book club, the charity you support or the political party for which you vote. You can also be a part of a certain system as a result of a different choice, like the system of residents in your town or neighbourhood. It is even possible that you become part of a system against your will, like a system of traffic accident victims. Larger entities, such as society, a country, a belief or nature, can also be seen as systems, each with their own rules, codes, views, norms and values.

A system is not owned by anyone, it simply exists. It has no physical body, yet it does have its own identity, its own soul even. It behaves in its own way. The parts match the properties of the whole or might even copy them. You might show an entirely different sense of humour in one system than in another. It can be hard for a candidate who is not "blue" enough to become part of a blue system in which security and risk avoidance are of primary importance. It might not be a good idea to hire a candidate like that. However, sometimes a candidate like that is hired anyway. In that case a person is hired "to be a breath of fresh air", which is an impossible task. Employment gives the right to a position within the system. You can only be a breath of fresh air from outside the system.

There is one system that is always present and has a special place, whatever you do: the system of your family. In systemic jargon this is called your "system of origin". Other systems are added later, such as your social circle, schools, clubs, teams and organisations, but none of these are as evident and invariable as the system of your family and your place of birth. Sometimes this is against your will. Without this system, you would not have been born and you would not have become who you are today. In the first system – your system of origin – the foundation has been laid for your behaviour in other systems.

" *Your system of origin is leading.* **"**

SB   I'm the oldest of four daughters. My parents love each other and their four girls dearly. I grew up in the north of Holland, in a small village on the edge of the IJsselmeer. In my early youth we went to church every Sunday. My world was so small and protected that, until I was ten, I thought every child had a father and a mother, a home with a garden and a car. I made different choices as an adult. Choices that were the opposite of the experiences in my youth. My desire was to discover the world and the work I do as an adult woman enables this. When I became a mother, my husband and I decided to move from the city to a village. We now have a house, a beautiful garden and not one, but two cars. I can now go wherever I please. I'm happily repeating the pattern.

Being part of a system is also about you as a person. You carry parts of each of those different systems to which you belong with you. It is difficult to discover which parts are really you and which parts originate from the system. This does not matter. It is a fact that what you think, want and do sometimes has more to do with the system you are part of than with you as an individual. You might recognise the feeling of thinking, acting or talking as a "representative" of one of these systems, which shows how strong the connection is.

Every week when I do my shopping there's a homeless man selling street newspapers in front of the supermarket. I regularly feel the need to buy a paper from him. It's not that I like him that much, that the contents of the paper appeal to me, or that I feel guilty about my full shopping cart. I'm not exactly sure which system "calls" on me to contribute to his sales. What I do know is that it's self-evident; I don't have to think about it. It might have something to do with my uncle – my father's youngest brother – who lived in a homeless shelter for a while. All my cousins adored this handsome, somewhat eccentric uncle. So did I. Do I see my uncle at a soul level when I buy the paper? Is that why I feel more connected to the system of homeless shelters? Or am I connected to a larger system at that moment, a system that stands for equal opportunities in society?

LS

In this book we mainly focus on the system in which you take part as a working professional: the organisational system. It is impossible to look at this system without including your family system from time to time. Your identity as a professional is largely influenced by experiences and events from your family system, your past and the way you have handled your past and your survival strategies. Every day you take yourself, and all these experiences from your personal history, with you to work. It often happens that the opinions and patterns from your family system dominate the organisational context, without you realising this.

1.3 Family systems

When you are born you gain your own place within the family system. This place is a given fact. You did not choose it and you cannot escape it. Your place within your family system is part of your human existence and is thus existential. There were generations before you and there might be many generations after you. You will unconditionally be a part of your family system.

SB My grandmother didn't make it easy for her children to love her. Over the course of her entire life she made choices that had a negative effect on the well-being of every member of the family. In 2014 she passed away at the age of eighty-nine. I often asked my mother why she kept visiting and taking care of my grandmother, in spite of all the old and new pain she was exposed to again and again. The answer was always the same: *"She's my mother and I have to accept that, with all the pain that goes with it. She's the only mother I have."*

In the family system we speak of "place" (instead of "position" as we do in organisational systems). Your place in this system is a fact and cannot be replaced. You are not replaceable either. You are born as the child of your father and mother; you will have no other (biological) parents. You are the first, second, third or umpteenth child in a line of brothers and sisters. The order within the family system is clear, everyone knows who has been part of the system the longest, who is older and who is younger.

SB After my grandmother's death my oldest aunt took charge. As the first child in the family she felt that it was her task to organise the funeral and divide my grandmother's humble possessions. This felt natural for the other sisters and they accepted her in this role, in spite of wanting to make different choices themselves. The task of organising the cremation and settling the inheritance "belonged" to the oldest child in this system. Who had taken care of my grandmother during her illness didn't make any difference in this order.

Living and surviving are at the core of the family system. From a systemic perspective the only objective of a family system is passing on the gift of life to the next generation. If this does not happen the family will go extinct. In this respect it is easy for people with children because they have literally passed on the gift of life. People without children, intentionally and unintentionally, pass life on to the next generations in other ways. You often see these people investing their passion and talents in their work, hobbies or charities.

My parents are grandparents to eleven grandchildren. Of course they're all equally special. One grandchild is extra special: the first one. Due to the birth of this child they became grandparents, causing them to "move up a generation". This child confirms that life has been passed on.

SB

Love and connection are the biggest forces within the family system, but that does not say anything about the form in which that love and loyalty are expressed. The order within the family system is clear. Parents go before children, the elder children go before the younger ones. Of course parents can use their power for their own gain in their children's upbringing, but usually love and connection are leading forces within a family.

The news that my father was ill came from nowhere. Cancer. Without us having to say or organise anything, my sisters and I came together. We sat at a table full of good food, like we do in our family. There we were, with all our differences, our busy lives with young children and our demanding jobs. It was natural and unconditional. We shared our shock, our worries and our love for each other and especially for my father.

SB

" You get a family system, you choose an organisational system. "

1.4 Organisational systems

People join organisational systems voluntarily. Every day you have the choice to stay or not, even though it might not literally feel like that. It works the same the other way around: the organisation can choose to offer you a job, extend your contract or terminate your contract, whatever the reason. Your place within the organisation is usually temporary. Your "residence time" at an organisation is conditional and is based on a quid-pro-quo principle.

LS I worked in sales at a pharmaceutical company for six years and I had the ambition to grow further. A colleague was going to retire in the near future. I had the best qualifications to take his position, which matched my ambitions perfectly. I was waiting for my chance. Then the parent company decided that the position would be eliminated. There went my vision of the future. The quid-pro-quo principle I felt for this organisation didn't apply anymore. My time was up. I took responsibility and started following a postgraduate training degree on my own time, with my own money. I prepared myself for the next step: outside of this organisation.

Within organisations we speak of a "position" (instead of a "place" as we do in family systems). Positions within organisational systems change in many different ways. Positions can be added or removed. They are replaceable. Within these positions, the employees can also change. Everyone in the organisation is replaceable and interchangeable. If people feel that this is not the case there might be a system disorder. These people are usually looking from the perspective of a family system. However, a position within the organisational system is not personal. The only exception is the position of the founder: this person is always part of the system and comes first. Without him or her, the company would never have existed in the first place.

LS I first visited the company at the exact moment that one of the two founders/directors was leaving. The man I went to talk with was going to continue on his own. It was important to him to make clear to both the employees and the clients that the split was amicable and that the organisation would remain ambitious and healthy. The departure was carefully thought through, as was the announcement to the staff. They had felt that there was something going on, but didn't know what. When the news got out they were initially shocked. At the farewell party, the remaining founder hung up a photo "from the beginning". It showed both founders, twenty years younger, proudly posing in front of their first office. After seeing that the departing director was granted a literal, permanent position in the organisation the employees settled down.

An organisation cannot exist without power. The question is not whether there is power, but how the organisation uses that power. If people in powerful positions do not take their influence and responsibility seriously it will be difficult to work towards their goal in an effective way. It is important for executives to truly accept the level of influence – and thus the power – that comes with a specific position and use it to reach their goal. This will also contribute to the right order within the organisation.

Hester is a team leader in a new organisation that was formed after a major reorganisation. *"Tell me what you'd like to do"*, Hester said during a team meeting. *"What is important to you and where shall we start?"* An uncomfortable silence settled over the room and everyone stared at the floor. When Hester asked why there was so little response, one of the team members replied that she had expected Hester to present her vision and objectives. This would provide the team with a clear direction and a framework for the future. Once Hester took the lead and told her team which way they would be going, they breathed a sigh of relief. Knowing where they stood gave them a platform to work towards their objectives, each from their own position.

Every organisation, department, team, position, brand, product and so on was once founded for a reason. The systemic term for this reason for being is "purpose".

The purpose is the answer to the question: "Why was this product made?" The core task that must be achieved to reach this purpose determines the organisation's main objective. If the organisation loses sight of this core task, it will also lose focus and direction. This sometimes occurs within organisations where people focus more on mutual interaction than on their tasks.

SB

Every now and then I'm offered a job. I sometimes fantasise about starting an agency and hiring people. It never takes long for me to go back to my main purpose: freedom. I'm self-employed because I want to be free. I immediately feel that it wouldn't be the right choice for now, but I'm sure that one day my current purpose of being self-employed will be attained.

In family businesses there are other factors. The purpose is often continuity. Passing the business on to the next generation is often more important than making a profit. Family businesses take fewer risks and try to remain as independent from banks as possible. This contributes to continuity. Selling property such as land or buildings only happens if the family does not need these now or in the future. It is only done when absolutely necessary to make a quick profit. The family system and the organisational system are intertwined in family businesses. The existence of the family and of the business is so closely linked that there is no actual distinction between the two. As an employee of a family business this is noticeable. The ever-present question is: "*Where do I stand?*" You will also always remain an outsider in comparison to the ones belonging to the family.

Herbert was a manager at a large and successful catering establishment. He had made some vague agreements about taking over the business from the couple who owned it. Those agreements had been made eight years ago. The owners never made any signs of actually discussing the transfer of ownership. One

day a new manager was introduced: the twenty-two year old son of the owners who had just dropped out of university. He had no clue how to run a catering business, hired staff for the wrong reasons, was too late with his orders, in short: he didn't do very well. These kinds of mistakes had been reason enough to fire other people in the past. The son stayed. Herbert felt it was time to pack his bags. He wanted to run his own business and he realised that, in spite of his good work, he could not prevail over the family's own son.

1.5 Conscience: communicating with the larger whole

Using your systemic wisdom means working with the larger whole. Through symptoms in the overcurrent, the separate parts show what is needed in the whole. For example, if an organisation shows a large turnover of staff you can look into making changes in employment and working conditions. That would mean looking at a part of the whole. From a systemic perspective the employee turnover is (also) seen as a part of a larger whole, a part of the entire organisational system for example. In order to learn to recognise and discuss these influences – which are constantly present within yourself, your team or your organisation – it is essential to understand how conscience works. The term conscience is open to many interpretations. In this context it is sufficient to explain the two most important types of conscience: the group conscience and the systemic conscience. People in organisations constantly act on these types of conscience. Sometimes this even happens subconsciously and goes against their own beliefs.

"Hey Siets, you coming to the pub?" In the organisation where I worked it was normal to discuss business in the pub on Friday afternoon, after working hours. I was about to leave for home, to see my family. I knew that saying "*no*" would mean that I would be less connected to the organisation, making my job harder. I do enjoy having a drink from time to time. On the other hand I knew my family would be disappointed if I said "yes" to drinks. Besides, I had also made a resolution to go for an intensive workout the next day.

SB

" *Conscience works like an extra sense.* "

Bert Hellinger – the founder of the systemic phenomenological approach and constellations – describes conscience as an extra sense that allows you to register what to do to belong to a group. And once you belong to the group, your conscience tells what your place within the group is and what is expected of you. Conscience is a sense, just like your sense of balance. If you lose your sense of balance you become dizzy. This is an unpleasant feeling, so you correct your stance. This mainly happens subconsciously. That is also how your conscience works. If you observe the unwritten rules of the group's conscience, you can join in. If you act differently than the rest of group, you risk being excluded. Or you might not fit in properly because you show a different type of behaviour than is expected of you.

Just like your inner ear can make you experience dizziness, your conscience can make you feel guilty. You then have a "guilty conscience", even though it might be subtle or only last briefly. As a human you constantly encounter the barriers of your conscience. You are loyal – consciously and subconsciously – to the systems you belong to, the systems you support or the ones you identify with strongly. The system that influences the formation of your conscience the most is your family of origin: the family in which you grew up.

SB

"No, I'm not coming", I said. It felt both good and unpleasant at the same time. *"Come on, don't be boring!"* I felt my body react immediately and a knot started to form in my stomach. *"I'd love to"*, I said, *"but I want to pick up my oldest son from judo."* As soon as I had spoken those words the knot in my stomach disappeared. I realised which system was most important for me.

People cannot survive on their own. Every human feels the urgent basic need to belong somewhere, to be part of a group. The group conscience provides the "rules", it prescribes the type of behaviour that fits within the group and the type that does not. It teaches us what to do to fit in. The group conscience allows you to instinctively decide what is right and what is wrong. The first group conscience you face is that of the family you grow up in. Doing something "wrong" -- breaking the rules and doing something differently than "usual" -- will make you feel guilty. This mainly happens subconsciously. Later on in life, when you start to reflect on yourself, you become more conscious of how the group conscience functions.

For my birthday I received a carefully wrapped present from a dear friend. Everyone watched me unwrapping my gift. It turned out to be a colourful scarf. My friend told me that if I didn't like it, she would be happy to keep it herself. As it turned out, I didn't particularly like the scarf... The opportunity to swap my gift was laid out for me, however, I immediately felt guilty. This feeling originated from the group conscience of my family. I was taught at a young age "*not to look a gift horse in the mouth*". At the same time I thought of the group conscience of my friends present: what would they think of me if I were honest about the scarf? According to the mores of my group of friends, was being honest "done" or "not done"? Would it make me belong more or less? I felt the tendency to choose the easiest way out and thank my friend for her gift. But then I re-alised that I would feel guilty too, towards myself. My friend also deserved an honest answer. It didn't feel right to say "*No, it's beautiful*", so after a few seconds I said that I would like to swap it for a different one. Either way I wouldn't have been able to answer without feeling guilty.

LS

Later on in life there are other groups (or systems, to be precise) with their own social rules, habits and codes of conduct that determine whether and to what extent you fit in. This can be a group of friends but also an organisation, club, neighbourhood or country.

When you are loyal to the group conscience -- by acting in the way expected of you -- it feels "innocent" in a way. It gives you the right to belong to the group. Behaving differently will make you fit in less. De-velopment -- whether it is the development of a teenager or that of a team -- is inextricably linked to feeling guilty. Are you prepared to feel guilty to do what is necessary? And if you choose to always remain innocent, can you still live your life to the full?

A large part of human action comes from the group conscience. You do whatever is necessary to fit in with the group, even though this happens mostly subconsciously. Every group or system has its own group conscience. Which conscience motivated the attack on the satirical magazine Charlie Hebdo? Seen from their position within their group, were the attackers guilty or innocent? Did it make them fit in more or less? And what about that commercial director? The one that received praise from within his own organisation for that smart move which drove the competitor out of business? He also acted from a clean group conscience and feels innocent. His actions confirm his position within the organisational system.

There is also a different kind of conscience. This kind surpasses the boundaries of time and space. It is not tangible or audible and functions in the subconscious. Its name is the "systemic conscience". The systemic conscience safeguards the survival of the system as a whole. It transcends right and wrong, does not consider what should or should not be and is not affected by trends and opinions. You can think of the systemic conscience as a collective memory for the whole system. Within this conscience, the individual is subordinate to the whole system. Sometimes a person is "employed" by the systemic conscience. This happens completely subconsciously. If an employee or a team fails to perform to an acceptable standard without any identifiable reasons, it is possible that this person or group has been employed by the systemic conscience. By this we mean that he must identify something for the benefit of the larger whole. That is why the systemic conscience is also known as the collective conscience.

LS During an intake for a team training I spoke to the new head of the finance department. He told me that there had been eight managers in this department in the past five years. From my systemic knowledge I asked if there had been any special departures in the past. The answer was yes. Five years ago the then department head -- who was very popular with the staff -- had reported sick in response to a conflict with the management about the enormous amount of pressure at work. The board had settled the case financially and that was that. Nobody had the chance to say goodbye to the department head. None of his successors held the function for long. One became ill, the other received a better offer elsewhere and a third started his own company. It was like they weren't able to stay in that position. This organisation's systemic conscience needed to say farewell to the former department head. Only then would the position be vacant at a deeper level and would it be possible for someone to take the position. The new head organised a meeting with the staff. They told him everything about the departed manager. He connected with the former department head on LinkedIn and the staff sent him a card saying how sorry they felt about the way he had left and that they hoped he was doing alright. Finally the position was truly "free".

When a person shows behaviour originating from the systemic conscience it does not make sense to give this person feedback. He is simply not able to behave differently. Even if he does succeed in changing his habits, someone else will carry on with the (unwanted) behaviour. After all, the behaviour stems from something larger than the person. In the example above, the department heads who had left were certainly good at their job. Attention had certainly been paid to a sufficient selection procedure. However, the position within the organisational system was in a sense still "taken" because the former head had left without saying goodbye. The systemic conscience is persistent. As soon as you see a pattern emerge it is worthwhile to look into the life-giving forces in the undercurrent. What is being overlooked that belongs to the system? How is the balance between taking and giving? What is the order within the system?

1.6 System energy: the nature of a system

Every system has its own "system energy". The system energy is not about the individuals within the system, although you can recognise the energy in each one. All people, and animals too, have an innate antenna for system energy.

New York feels completely different than Los Angeles. This can be noticed immediately in the pace and the atmosphere of everyday life. The people who live in New York can vary from each other in all possible ways, but when it comes to the feel of the city it is completely different to "be a New Yorker" than to "be an Angeleno".

New York's system energy is different to the system energy of Los Angeles. Everyone can sense and confirm this, without even knowing anything about these cities. Your antenna for system energy tells you how to connect to a system, what is important in a system and what the behavioural rules are. As an individual it is entirely up to you to which information provided by the system energy you respond. However, the system energy can direct your choice, decide what you conform to and show which behavioural rules and codes apply.

" *People have an innate antenna for system energy.* "

System energy can be compared with an atom. An atom consists of three parts: protons, neutrons and electrons. Together with the neutral neutrons the protons form the core of the atom. Around that core there is a cloud of electrons. These electrons have no fixed place and can be described as charged energy that moves around the core as a result of the attraction to the protons. System energy can be compared to that cloud of electrons: it is always present and without it, the system does not really exist. It is not tangible, identifiable or provable, but it is there.

LS   I visited a commercial organisation for an acquisition talk. Twenty years ago I was an employee in the sales department of this company. In the meantime the company had moved several times, the product range had changed completely and there was almost nobody left from my time at the company and yet it felt so familiar when I walked in! Almost like coming

home. The vibe, the look and the organisation culture were the same as twenty years before. The separate parts of this organisational system had changed completely through the years; yet the organisation as a whole felt the same.

Exercise – Describing System Energy   *Application 1*

This exercise will help you learn to describe system energy and provide a language for what you already know in your subconscious.

1. Name three systems that you belong to yourself. How would you describe each system's energy?

2. Is the energy of these different systems similar?
   What does that mean?

3. To what extent do you (and your own system energy) match certain organisations?

An organisation's system energy shows the best qualities of the organisation. Which characteristics are well developed? To what aspects does the organisation give time and attention? The characteristics that are emphasised form the face of the company, both internally and externally. This automatically means that other characteristics are pushed to the background and ignored. If an organisation succeeds in incorporating these characteristics too, there are huge benefits to be gained, like vitality, productivity and job satisfaction. The organisation will be better balanced. The system will become more "whole".

I arrive at the pharmaceutical company for my appointment. The lobby is enormous and there's a modern, wooden front desk with a well-groomed receptionist. The lobby seems even larger due to its minimalistic and tasteful decoration: a single trendy seating area, a huge vase of fresh flowers and a piece of modern art. While I'm waiting I receive a cappuccino with a luxury bonbon and a glass of water. I see a couple of employees passing. They're all attractive, chatting happily, and dressed according to the latest fashion. It's clear to me that an eye for style is a strong point in this organisation, it shows in everything. This company's system energy is focused on "creating

LS

---

the perfect picture". This is important information and it's essential that I match this energy if I want to work together with this organisation. At the same time I suspect that the growth potential lies in the opposite of this characteristic: accepting imperfections and flaws. I'm not sure what I can or will do with this information, but I keep it at the back of my mind during my appointment.

Application 2   *Exercise – Meeting a system*

This exercise is suitable for a first meeting with a system, whether an organisation, a team, a city, a country or a family. During that first meeting you expose yourself to the system's energy as much as possible. You can achieve that by opening up to all stimuli. Use your whole body as a projection screen. The organisation's system energy will then flow through you.

1. Begin with the intention, the wish to meet the system and everything that goes with it. The achievements, the failures, the things to be proud of, the things that people prefer to keep hidden. Allow yourself to be guided by genuine interest. Judgements, opinions and being right will not help you here. If you realise that you are passing judgement, note this and realise that it is interesting that you have this judgement. Nothing more, nothing less.

2. Start easy, by observing. Use all your senses. Open them up. Pay attention to the language used. How do people communicate? When communicating, is there a connection? How is the location decorated?

3. Take it a step further. What do you notice? How do people move here? To what do they pay attention? What is funny or remarkable about this system?

4. The next step is more in-depth and focuses more on experience than on observation. How does it feel being here? What stands out? Is there something missing that you might have expected? Are there things you recognise from one of the systems you belong/have belonged to? If you belonged to this system, would you be conflicted or would it feel like coming home? Where in your body can you sense that?

Imagine yourself as a membrane. There is no filter for things to become stuck in, only a membrane through which everything can pass. Allow the system energy to flow through you and feel what it is exactly that is passing through you. Nothing stays behind; everything flows through.

Every time you enter a place for the first time you meet a new system. Whether it is a client, an introduction to someone new, a country you are visiting or a company to which you are applying. Your innate antenna lets you know and feel how things work there. This happens subconsciously. You are particularly sensitive to system energy when you meet the system for the first time. Once you visit a place more often this sensitivity fades. That is because the system energy becomes more "ordinary", because you have (increasingly) become part of the system. From within the system you make different observations than from "outside". With some practice it is possible to quickly improve your antenna for system energy. This will allow you to gain more information about the system you are working with.

I had been asked to organise an afternoon for a group of twenty experienced lawyers. The afternoon was part of a programme focusing on cooperation. The lawyers were sitting at a long table, with me at the head. They all had pen and paper in front of them. They were chatting animatedly and clever little jokes were thrown back and forth. It was like a game of wit. How would I get these people to work on cooperating? I focused on my breathing and heart rate and quietly looked at every person at the table. When it was silent for a moment I asked everyone to move their chair back one metre. Surprised, they did what I asked. A deeper silence and sense of peace settled over the room. All of a sudden, it was as if there was a real connection between the people present. From this different system energy it was interesting to work on improving cooperation.

SB

The better you are at identifying the system energy, the easier your work will be. It will become easier to understand what exactly is going on. You can connect to the organisational system by checking the system energy, without having to be a part of the system yourself. At that moment you can access the information coming both from inside and from outside the system. Listen to the language used by your conversation partners. How do they talk about clients? Are they seen as sources of income or are the clients seen as the people who enable the organisation's existence? How do they talk about competitors? Should these be crushed or is there only playful tension?

After discovering the nature of the system energy you can ask the right questions and find out which hypotheses would be relevant to test.

1.7 Constellations and systemic work

Systemic work has become known because of the constellation technique. The best known are the family and organisation constellations. During a constellation people take the place of humans, events or other important elements that play a role in an issue or problem. These people, called representatives, connect to the information and the feelings attached to the relevant system. A constellation immediately gives form to system energy. Everyone who experiences this for the first time is surprised by how easily and strongly the system energy can be observed. This is because system energy does not rely on time and place. When you take a place in a constellation as a representative it is like "logging in on the Wi-Fi network" of the relevant system, even if you are at a different location and working with different people.

As a spectator or representative in a constellation it is easy to observe the system energy. You resonate on the already existing connections. There is no need to learn any special skills or follow a certain procedure.

The type of observation we mean here requires your full attention in the here and now. Sneaking a glance at your phone or making a mental shopping list is a no-go. Being fully present requires a wait-and-see attitude. There is no need to help or look for a solution. You just need to pay attention and be fully "present".

" *A constellation immediately gives form to system energy.* "

During the intake Luis told me that his colleagues accused him of not taking on his role as a project leader properly. I decided to ask about his background. He told me about his adoptive parents. He had never met his biological parents and wasn't interested in them either. I suggested a constellation. He didn't see the benefits at first, but he decided to take part anyway. Instantly he realised how warm his relationship with his biological parents was and how loyal he was to them. Luis was surprised at the intensity of his own feelings. I asked him to try and contact his biological parents and introduce them to his own children. Tears streamed down his face. After this meeting we ended the constellation.

Luis told me later that he felt more rooted and that feeling enabled him to do a better job as a project leader.

LS

Of course this way of observing is not restricted to constellations, which is the form for which systemic work has become known. You can adopt this attitude anywhere, at any time. This will help you adopt a different "state of being", in which you can welcome whatever it is that presents itself. Without knowing, without intentions, without plans. This attitude will help you come into contact with the system energy. It is like logging in on to the systemic conscience of the family or organisational system you are dealing with. You will surpass the level of individuality and connect to the knowledge and the memory of the whole system. You now have (better) access to all the information stored there. Opening up to the signals that reach you through the systemic conscience will immediately offer new options. These options are not devised in your head, but have developed from your systemic wisdom.

You are now ready to start your adventure through the rest of this book. Go with the flow. Read carefully, but do not feel the need to know or understand everything. Take the time to discover your systemic wisdom and develop it further, so you can add this to all the other things you already know, feel and do.

Knowing

2

" *Everything has a function for the whole.* "

In the systemic approach you do not zoom in on the problems that occur. A problem is seen as a manifestation – a symptom – of something going on at a deeper level. To find out what is truly going on you have to enter an observant state. You watch, feel and register, without forming an opinion or judgement. There is no right or wrong, better or worse. You pay attention to the different elements in the system, their mutual relationships and how they relate to the whole. In doing so, you assume that what you are observing has a function for the whole. Your starting point is that the problem, i.e. the symptom, is there for a reason. It is "a solution" for something going on in the system. The problem is nothing other than the best possible solution the system currently can provide.

Anja was a manager at a successful medical practice. Unfortunately, over the previous six months, the practice had begun to suffer losses for the first time. There were no external circumstances that could explain the losses. It was as if their patients had decided overnight that they preferred a different practice. The practice was owned by four specialists who had formed a partnership. Anja's salary was one and a half times larger than that of her partners. It had been exactly six months ago that her colleagues objected to this. They didn't think it fair that one of them earned more than the others. Anja wanted to address their objections and gave up part of her salary. She confessed that this drained her energy. She no longer felt the same drive as she used to feel. She preferred working with her own patients and no longer busied herself with management tasks or future plans. In her subconscious Anja felt that "she was balancing out her smaller salary by investing less". It was as if the patients could feel these changes in the atmosphere. They reacted to these changes by switching practices.

From a systemic perspective you pay more attention to the underlying patterns than to the individual problems. Once you start looking at systems that way you will find out that every system has its own story and its own patterns from which you can tell what kind of system it is. In other words: the character and temperament of that system. There are countless different systems. Through all the research and experience with systemic work -- first in families and later on in organisations -- it has become clear that there are universal laws that apply to every system. In this book we call them the life-giving forces of systems. In professional literature they are also known as systemic principles, systemic laws or the basic needs of the system.

2.1 The life-giving forces of systems

If the life-giving forces are fulfilled, an organisational system can function at its best. People enjoy their work, feel appreciated, are proactive and perform better. When a new initiative or idea does not work out it is a learning experience instead of a failure. Clients, suppliers or (local) media are attracted to the organisation and enjoy being part of the system in their own way. However, it also works the other way around: when the life-giving forces are not observed this has a negative effect. This can manifest itself in different ways: from going to work every day feeling stressed to a burnout. From slacking to deliberately and systematically committing fraud. In the worst case the system or the individuals within the system can become ill or even collapse.

Humans have an innate antenna for "what feels right and what does not" when it comes to the life-giving forces. They intuitively act according to those feelings. This can be painfully clear in the hospitality sector. In a square full of restaurants and bistros they are all full, except one. Even when looking closely, it is hard to tell why that restaurant is empty. We call the manifestation of this behaviour showing on the outside -- the empty restaurant -- the overcurrent. In a family's overcurrent these manifestations can be recurrent quarrels, forms of depression or certain events such as accidents. In an organisation's overcurrent these manifestations can be vacancies that cannot be filled, staff committing fraud, and continuing reorganisations.

The invisible, indefinable psychological process is situated in the undercurrent. Just like the response of the people in the square, who appar-

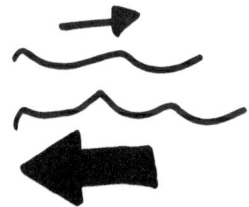

ently all choose to avoid one restaurant but would not be able to explain why when asked. According to some the undercurrent is not predictable or impressionable. However, from a systemic perspective the undercurrent is highly predictable and definitely impressionable, especially when you know more about systems and the life-giving forces that apply to each system.

From a systemic perspective the symptom -- the thing that appears in the overcurrent -- is a sign that there is a disturbance in the undercurrent: a life-giving force has not been fulfilled. This is certainly true when it comes to problems or situations that reoccur in various forms or over several generations. In such a case you can assume that there is an explanation in the undercurrent. That also means there is a solution. A professional trained in the systemic method will always look for what is happening in the undercurrent. The symptoms in the overcurrent are simply an indication, a starting point from which to continue your search. These professionals increasingly use constellations because this is a fast and effective way to make the undercurrent visible.

LS The very first coaching group of my career as a trainer consisted of six people from a small support service department within a college. They were all slightly older and came for a two-day training course in Personal Effectiveness. It couldn't have been clearer that they were sent by their manager. Right at the beginning of the training I met a lot of resistance, complaining and disinterest. I tried really hard to turn things around. I showed understanding, I confronted them, I thought of fun exercises. Nothing worked. At the end of the day I was exhausted. I had worked extremely hard to take away all the resistance and negativity in the overcurrent. Afterwards I called to inform my client about my day and my experiences. It was only then that I heard about problems in the undercurrent: the department had been formed a couple of years earlier as a sort of "collection" of people that weren't useful to any other part of the organisation. They were employees who were either too expensive to dismiss or who did not function properly elsewhere. That was the group I was dealing with. These people's positions had been "invented" to give them something to do. These positions had no additional value to the organisational system.

The "support service" component of the system was overfull and that was the reason for the lack of energy within this part of the organisation. No wonder that these six people gave the impression of being so jaded: they had been discarded by the organisation and that showed in the undercurrent. I decided to cancel the second day of the training course. There was nothing I could do for these people in regard to personal effectiveness. The undercurrent clearly showed the limits of the possibilities.

2.2 Belonging

You might have experienced it yourself: you are at a funeral or cremation and one family member is not mentioned. All members of the family are welcomed as they should be, except that one sister. She is not mentioned. Even though that sister is not present, even though no one likes that sister: it is extremely painful that she is ignored. Everyone present can sense that things are not as they should be. This is due to the life-giving force of "belonging".

" *Why that family member who is never mentioned will always be part of the family.* "

Every system strives towards completeness. If there are people, functions, products or events which are excluded or not acknowledged the whole system becomes weaker. This can show through all kinds of symptoms that become visible in the overcurrent, such as gossiping, reduced efforts, self-justification, or negativity in the form of complaining. The symptoms visible in the overcurrent are a direct reflection of the deeper disturbances in the undercurrent and therefore show what is really going on.

I worked on an interim basis for an organisation whose policy it was to work with external staff as little as possible. The assign-   **SB** ment was to help steer them through a large reorganisation. Working for this company was highly complicated. On the one hand they truly appreciated my contribution and I was the one requested for this assignment. On the other hand I wasn't really wanted because I wasn't a permanent member of staff. I noticed this act of "excluding", which was present in the undercurrent, in all kinds of signals in the overcurrent. For example, it took four weeks before I received an email address, while this only took two days for new employees. My invoices weren't paid on time either: there was simply no proper procedure when it came to hiring external workers. When I wanted to take on my responsibilities and perform my tasks, I was often told: *"Maybe someone else should do it."* In the fifteen months that I was working for this organisation it was as if the brakes were always on. I was constantly asking myself whether I was wanted or not. Was I allowed to be here or not? This feeling cost me lots of energy, energy that I couldn't dedicate to the work I was doing.

The rule is simple really: everyone connected to the system is entitled to a position. As a member of the system you have contributed to the system. For better or for worse, the system would not be the same without this contribution.

Because systems do not function in a linear or circular way, time and place have no influence. This approach also includes people or events from the past in the system. The founder of the organisation and the people who made the starting capital available will always belong to the system. Without them, the system would not exist. In the system "being Dutch" the Second World War will always have a place, as will Indonesia and Suriname. This also applies to building dikes and pumping "the polders" dry. There is no nation on earth as good at reaching a consensus as the Dutch. We have to; otherwise there would be no way we could live on this part of the earth, which is literally under water. It is all part of the system of "being Dutch", even though a Dutch person might not directly have anything to do with it. This also explains why it is so difficult to migrate. The system you grow up in is the most important one; it shapes you. The family and the surroundings you grew up in: that is your definition of home, no matter how you experienced it. All the other moments and surroundings that will become your home later on in life are different from that first one. From a systemic perspective it is only possible for someone to integrate when they acknowledge their origin and the new country accepts this too.

People, events, values, beliefs, dreams, concepts: they can all be part of a system. Not all parts are equally important. The parts that are essential to the system's survival are the most important ones. That means almost automatically that events or people who lie further in the past are less important. Instead of players in the field, these people or events become supporters in the stands. Yet they still belong to the system: it is no real match without the supporters. In the theory of family systems it is assumed that family members up to seven generations back still influence the current system. The ones who you know or have known personally -- such as parents, grandparents and maybe even great-grandparents -- have a greater influence than the ones who came before. Still, events and experiences from people from earlier generations appear to have a continuous influence in the current family system.

As an individual it can be hard to acknowledge that something or someone belongs to the system, especially when this event of this person is causing you to be annoyed. For example, a brother or sister who always takes and never gives in return and therefor causes an imbalance or a manager who is above you, while you have to sit back and watch all the mistakes he or she makes. Or much worse: acknowledging that an accident that your organisation has caused -- with human victims as a result -- belongs to the organisation's system.

Belonging does not mean agreeing with, approving of or wanting everything that makes up the system. Belonging, in the systemic meaning of the word, means accepting that something is part of the system; whether you like it or not. It is given its own place within the whole. You can recognise it as part of the system. Belonging is felt in the heart, not in the head. An empowering thought is: "it is the way it is and I must accept that", especially in situations in which trauma or guilt play a large role.

A specialised production company – founded by two friends – had only been in business for a couple of years when one of the partners died. He hadn't followed the safety instructions on

---

the machine he was working with. The fatal accident happened in the factory, in the presence of his partner and a few employees. It was a traumatic experience, for all those involved. The other partner wanted to carry on with the business and sat down with the parents of his deceased friend to discuss buying out his partner's share. With the help of a specialist it was decided that the father of the deceased would remain co-owner for the following five years. He came to the company every day and did all kinds of chores. The deceased partner, friend and son was honoured with photos, stories and anecdotes during lunch. On his birthday and the date of his death they always lit a candle. The company became a huge success. The organisation could remain alive, thanks to the acceptance of death.

Sometimes there are secrets in a system. These secrets stem from a feeling of shame or guilt. Think of an accident that need not have happened. A classic situation in an organisation is the director having an affair with his secretary. In families the most frequent secrets have to with a family member committing a crime or having a different sexual orientation. In the overcurrent the secret can remain a secret. Whoever enters the system after the event will not know about it. When it comes to the undercurrent it is a different story altogether. A secret will always be tangible there. There is something going on, even though you do not know what exactly. The secret prevents the system from developing freely. The presence of something unwelcome, something that does not belong, demands attention and thus gains more "power". Compare it with a telephone that keeps ringing, but is not picked up.

At Alcoholics Anonymous (AA) the life-giving force of belonging is applied perfectly. Everyone introduces themselves by name and says: "*I am an alcoholic.*" For many people alcoholism is an addiction that they hide from the outside world. By saying that you're an alcoholic out loud, you acknowledge the addiction. The idea behind this is that accepting the problem makes it manageable instead of being something that you are subjected to. The AA organisation also uses belonging in another way. On their website they say: "*To be sure of sobriety, alcoholics simply have to stay away from alcohol*". This means that

drinking alcohol must be completely excluded. However, AA is systemically smart about the way it presents this exclusion by using the "just for today" meditation. This is based on the following intention: *"Just for today I will try to live through this day only, and not tackle my whole life problem at once. I can do something for 12 hours that would appal me if I felt I had to keep it up for a lifetime."* **With this intention the AA organisation includes alcohol in their system.**

A secret in systemic sense does not necessarily have to be revealed. Neither does a trauma have to heal completely. Systemically, it is important that the members of the system recognise that there is a secret or trauma. Acknowledging it is sufficient. Additionally, it is important that the members, considering their place within the system, realise that it is not up to them to do or think something about it.

In summary: every system strives towards completeness. Systems that are not complete suffer from development issues and energy loss. Being complete means including everything and everyone who has contributed to the system. Large or small, important or less important, everything and everyone belongs. Acknowledging this is enough.

Exercise – An Image of your Family System   *Application 3*

Make a two or three-dimensional image of your family system.

- You can make a drawing, with circles stating people's names. Post-its can be handy too: you can write on them and move them around.

- Another option is using an empty table with items such as glasses, cups, tea bags, Playmobil dolls, wooden blocks, game pieces et cetera. These can be used to represent different parts of the system.

Representing your family system visually allows you to immediately see to which bigger whole you belong and who else is part of it. If you then go through the questions below you can identify the unconscious influences from your system of origin. Maybe you can already differentiate between what is your own and what you took from your family system. Increasing this awareness offers you more freedom of choice: what do I want and what do I not want (anymore)? This can increase your freedom of movement to choose your own path.

1. Start with yourself and your current living conditions, whether with a partner or family or not. Who belongs to this system? Who does not?

2. Continue by looking at the family you grew up in, your system of origin. What does it look like? Which values, views, and messages belong to this system?

3. Look back one generation. From which systems did your parents originate? In which way do you recognise these in the way you were raised?

4. You know this family system well from your own place. Try literally looking at it from a different perspective, for example by sitting at the other side of the table or standing up. What becomes visible now that was not visible before? You can also ask someone to look over your shoulder and listen to what stands out to him or her.

2.3 Order

" *Why twins always make it known who is the oldest within the first 30 minutes.* "

SB

I'm the oldest of four children. When my mother is in an affectionate mood she always calls me her "firstborn". That has always given me a special sense of comfort and security. My sisters still don't appreciate it when my mother says this in their presence. This type of affection is reserved for one person only and isn't interchangeable, however hard they try. My own family consists of six children, of which three were premature and died at birth. I could never call my oldest son my firstborn. According the life-giving force "belonging" there are six children. According the life-giving force "order" my son is third in line.

The order within a family is pretty simple. There is a natural, hierarchical order with a corresponding responsibility. The ones that come first are higher up in the order. That is why twins always let you know who is the older of the two: that way the order is clear for everyone.

Grandparents go before parents, parents before children, and children before grandchildren. This is the vertical order. When children fill up the place of (one of) the parents this causes a disturbance in the order, weakening all those involved. The same goes for parents behaving like their children's friends. Instead of maintaining the "parent spot" they take up a spot next to their children. The order within a family system is a natural boundary between the parents' domain and the children's domain.

In your family of origin your spot between your brothers and sisters is also fixed. Deceased children also keep their place in line. You are the first, second, third or umpteenth child of your parents. This is the horizontal order.

LS When my grandmother died my oldest aunt – who was eighteen at the time – filled in the role of mother. She took care of the youngest children and suddenly was in charge of the household and life at the farm. From a systemic perspective she filled in the place next to her father. From that moment onwards she left her own place as a child. Only when she was much older did she realise that she was the oldest daughter, even though she had to act as the mother. That was the way it was.

When it comes to in-laws the ordering principle of age does not work. The intensity of the connection is then more important than age. When you marry, you do not simply marry a person, you accept the entire system of that person's family: whatever has happened in the past, whatever is happening now. This can be difficult and sometimes people tend to refuse it: "*I am marrying you but I have my own family.*" The message in the undercurrent is then: "*I do not accept your family and thus I do not entirely accept you.*"

After a divorce, an ex-partner often remains part of the family system, especially when children have been born in the context of the marriage. Belonging to the system does not mean that you are obliged to actively keep in touch. It does mean that you acknowledge that the other was once important to you and helped make you who you are today. Adoption is a good example. The biological parents are first in order, the adoptive parents second. Without the biological parents the child would not exist in the first place. Acknowledging that this is true, however painful, brings peace to both the adopted child and the adoptive parents.

In organisational systems, on an archetypical level, certain functions can be compared to the roles and places within a family. Managers can be seen as parents, employees as children, teammates as brothers and sisters, interim managers as stepfathers and stepmothers. In making this comparison you get a feeling for the fitting hierarchical relations within the organisation. The order within organisations is slightly more complicated. Lots of different types of order are interwoven. The hierarchy is usually the dominant way of structuring the order. The people that are "higher up" have a bigger influence on the whole through the tasks and responsibilities that belong to the position. That automatically means that this person is more often right than his subordinates, because of his position. Even though he might not actually be right, this is how it works in the undercurrent. This is functional because it clearly shows where decisions are made.

Judith worked in a psychiatric health care team. When her team leader accepted a different job, she applied for that position and was hired. To her surprise everything changed immediately. Colleagues with whom she had once discussed strategies now asked her for instructions. "*I don't understand*", she said. "*I'm still the same Judith, but they act as if I'm a different person.*"

Your position within the organisational system is not fixed as it is in the family system. Someone can have different positions in various contexts, for example as chairman of the works council and a senior member of staff in their daily work. It matters whether you have a temporary or a permanent contract at an organisation, whether you are an intern or retired, whether you are, or have been, a co-owner.

I was working as an external advisor for a client who was implementing a flexible workspace concept. There were eight workspaces available for every ten employees. The calculations on attendance were in theory correct; however, in reality there were often not enough workspaces. With my lower position in the order – because I wasn't a permanent employee – I felt that I should give up my workspace to a colleague with a permanent contract.

SB

There are also other criteria that play a role when it comes to order. Most people can remember the date they started working at their current organisation, just as almost everyone who has started their own company knows when this happened. Colleagues know which one of them has been working for the organisation or team the longest. Those who have worked for the company the longest have more right to speak than those who have just started. The people who have worked for longer have also made a larger contribution to the system, as it is today, whatever this contribution might be.

Quinty will retire within the coming year. When asked how long she's been doing this work she answers: *"Exactly ten years next week, but actually it's been seventeen years. I worked here for four years before that. I took two years off because I was ill and after that I was dismissed. I was rehired after a year."* **Strictly speaking she spent 14 years working at this organisation. However, from a systemic perspective she has been part of the organisational system for seventeen years. She never really left.**

Having certain competences can also count as a criterion. In a market with more providers than clients, the sales department is higher in order than the maintenance department. A technical company that highly values service places their technical field service higher in the order. A different form of a contribution as a measure of order is someone who has made a special effort for the company. When someone saves the company from going out of business, that person receives a high position in the order, even if he or she was not part of the system before.

With the passing of time other events occur within the system and this person moves to the background. However, people like this will always be part of the organisational system seeing that without them, the system would no longer exist.

Jochem has been working in sales support at a wholesaler for over ten years. His most important task has always been accepting and processing orders. He's very good at his job. At one point the management decided that more turnover should be generated from customer contact via telephone. The sales staff must now use a more commercial approach, which means that they have to contact clients with sales promotions via telephone. All of a sudden competences such as proactivity, performance orientation and empathy are a must. Jochem initially struggles with this. He senses a change in his role within the department. Two younger colleagues with excellent sales skills now occupy a leading role, even though they've only recently started working for the company. Their competences place them in a higher spot than some of their more experienced colleagues. However, Jochem also notices that the changed method has a positive effect on the cooperation with other departments. The sales support department is taken more seriously now that the department contributes to the turnover and growth of the organisation. This enables Jochem to accept the consequences for his own position more easily.

The order within the organisational system is not about the equality between people, but provides clarity about the different positions. When everyone takes their own position with the corresponding responsibilities, peace and stability ensue. Undermining someone's position because you do not think they deserve it weakens the entire system. That does not mean that you have to settle for your current position. You could be promoted, change functions, or leave the organisation. Nobody's function and position in the order is fixed eternally. There is constant, although sometimes subtle, movement.

Francien has asked Cengiz to research how to increase productivity in her team. Cengiz is an external advisor who Francien knows from her previous job. Francien confides in Cengiz and tells him that she's eight weeks pregnant. She's having a bit of a hard time: she is tired and has difficulty concentrating. Cengiz helps her where possible, for example taking her place as the chair during work meetings and joining Francien when she heads out to important clients. The productivity within the team drops and the staff members become unsettled. Problems that were previously solved independently are now ignored. Lunch breaks now last longer than before. When taking a coffee break staff members wonder out loud whom they should be listening to: is Cengiz or Francien in charge?

Exercise – Your Family System: zooming in   *Application 4*

In the previous exercise you looked into the people and things belonging to your family system. In this exercise you pick one part or layer of your family system, for example, a generation or all family members of one gender.

1. How did you initially order the members and parts of the system when you did not know anything about the concept "order"?

2. Order the members, in the part of your system that you've chosen, according to age. How do you feel when you look at this? To what extent does this order match reality?

3. Move to another position, somewhere you enjoy being. Reflect on your actions by asking yourself the following questions: where have I seen this movement before? Who am I loyal to when I move like this? (This is usually one of the parents)

Find out what the triggers are – in your family of origin and in your work environment – to leave your own place or position. What can you do or not do to return to your own place or position?

2.4 Exchange

> *" Why it feels awkward when you receive a present that is too large. "*

To maintain a healthy relationship it is important to receive about the same as what you give. In practically all relationships in our lives it is important that there is a fair balance between giving and receiving. Not directly and not in the same form, but there should be a rough balance over the entire line of exchange. In anthropology, this is called "reciprocity". Without this exchange the interaction would stagnate. This applies to all relationships: between brothers and sisters, in friendships, romantic relationships and in teams. This is the horizontal balance of giving and taking. Think of that one friend who you always have to call first. If it happens a few times, it does not really matter. However, when it continues to happen it will start to bother you. Saying this out loud can seem childish, but the fact remains that there is a disturbance in the balance between giving and receiving. It blocks the healthy flow of exchange in the friendship. Ideas, love, attention and energy can no longer flow freely.

SB

One of my best friends had a lot of money for a period in his life. He went out to dinner, to concerts and he wore nice suits. At the same time I had little money. I was relieved when at the end of each month my salary was transferred into my account. Seeing each other was becoming extremely complicated. He always paid for our dinners. When we saw an interesting book in a shop window, he bought it for me as a present. He sent me envelopes with two tickets for a concert. Our friendship was never as complicated as it was during that period. How could I ever thank him? How could I ever re-establish the balance in a fitting way? I then set a clear boundary. *"If you want to stay friends with me, don't give me any more presents and split the bill with me when eating at cheaper restaurants."* **After that, our friendship could develop further and we are still good friends to this day.**

The perfect state of balance is hardly ever achieved. It is not important either; the exchange is what it is all about, searching for the best possible balance for the current moment. Just like walking: from a physiological perspective it is a continuous correction of falling, a constant search for the next moment of balance.

There are many people that naturally enjoy giving to others. People can give material things, but also immaterial things such as attention, interest, help or care. The giver gives with the best intentions, but without realising that it can be awkward for the receiver. Limitless giving disrupts the possibility of free exchange. Before you know it you reach an area of "guilt and innocence" in the undercurrent.

There was a period of time when I offered the introductory workshop Storytelling for free. I liked the idea of everyone being able to take part and experience the same positivity as I had with storytelling. As long as enough people signed up for the follow-up course, which wasn't free, I was satisfied. The workshop was always fully booked. I even had to work with a waiting list. But when push came to shove lots of people cancelled or didn't even show up. It was extremely frustrating.

Then I realised what I was doing: I was creating a "debt" between the participants and me, a debt that they couldn't repay. Since then I charged a small fee for these kinds of workshops and the exchange was back again. I didn't have a waiting list anymore, but the workshops were more effective and I enjoyed them more.

LS

When the balance between giving and receiving tips too much to one side, it starts getting awkward. The exchange can no longer flow freely. As a receiver, you become indebted to the giver. This effect is strengthened if the giver never requests anything in return or never accepts something from you. People with "helper's syndrome" may recognise this pattern. They give large amounts of attention, love or support without asking for anything in return. They remain innocent in their giving. The true effect is the reverse: those who only give and cannot receive, place themselves above the other in the undercurrent. It is impossible for the other to settle the outstanding debt. That is why it is not possible to continue giving without taking or receiving anything in return and remain innocent. The helper is then guilty of disturbing a healthy exchange.

LS

> **When I borrow something from my neighbour and I come to return it, she always says she doesn't need it back. She refuses to take it. Sometimes it's only something small, like an egg or a carton of milk, and then I accept her refusal. She also borrows from me after all. However, sometimes she brings me some things from the wholesaler. In that case I don't settle for her "*Oh, leave it*" and I pay her back the full amount, even if she tries to refuse. This ensures that our exchange as neighbours can continue.**

There are also situations to which the opposite applies. People then feel that they receive too little in return for what they give. In organisations this can happen easily when employees work a lot of extra hours without being rewarded for their efforts. When the balance between giving and receiving is tipped for a longer period of time you can see people trying to restore it themselves, for example by appropriating certain "rights". This can show in the overcurrent as various symptoms: from gossiping at the coffee machine or arriving late to taking supplies from the storeroom. In the undercurrent you have now also reached the area of guilt and innocence.

SB

> **I was extremely satisfied. I was working on a great assignment with lots of stability at a time when my family really needed that. I was learning a lot as a professional and I was enjoying my work immensely. I was also happy about my rate. It was in balance with my contribution to the company. Until I saw the rate of my fellow advisor... His rate was much higher, even though I thought my contribution was much more important**

and the risk of damage carried by me was much higher. I still don't know whether his rate was too high or mine too low. After noticing this I was fully aware of the difference. I stopped working hours that I couldn't bill and was less flexible when it came to rearranging private appointments in order to reach deadlines.

People have an innate antenna for the right balance between giving and receiving. They naturally want to exchange, even though this exchange is much more complicated than simply receiving money and security in exchange for hours of work. When a new manager is introduced but the working conditions remain the same, the balance is often – subconsciously – under debate again. In the Dutch system of collective labour agreements (CAOs) for many years it was customary that salaries increased annually, even if it was only an adjustment for inflation. This increase has now been stopped in several sectors due to the financial crisis. Many employees are starting to feel that the system is unbalanced.

You can usually sense whether you are receiving too little or taking too much. In an organisation a tipped balance can develop for all kinds of reasons. Which team hasn't had a discussion about colleagues who disappear during the day to have a smoke? Or about that colleague who leaves early to pick up his children from childcare, leaving you to finish up? Or about the boss who has the habit of sending e-mails in the evening and at the weekend to which an immediate response is expected?

Jim is an intelligent, stubborn man. He has finished two courses of study at university cum laude, but he never got the hang of those mobile phones. Why would anyone want to be reachable at all times? Personally, he didn't have that many urgent issues. "Not having a mobile phone" almost became part of his identity. The development of the smartphone also passed him by. He had never felt the urge to check his e-mail in the tram. His friends intervened on his fortieth birthday. *"We can't ever reach you"* they said. *"You're never there when we go out for a drink because we can't text you."* All this time, Jim thought

a smartphone could only be used to make calls. He had completely missed the mobile phone revolution and all its new communication capabilities. Therefore there was no possibility for exchange anymore.

Systems, and thus also organisations, are always exchanging. These exchanges occur both inside and outside of the system, in which a system can be a branch, a company, a team, a profession et cetera. A healthy balance between giving and receiving does not only apply to a personal level, between staff. There is also a constant exchange between the organisation and its stakeholders, such as clients, suppliers, shareholders, the parent company and/or external advisors. On an even larger scale there is also exchange between an organisation and its competitors, (export) markets and physical surroundings, for example.

Application 5   *Exercise – Discovering Life-giving forces in a system*

Discover your sensitivity for the life-giving forces with this simple exercise. Look at the website of a large organisation that is frequently in the news, for example a ministry, an environmental or human rights organisation, a (healthcare) institution or a large business group.

- Read the text on the website from a systemic perspective, without forming an opinion or judgement, an interest or goal. Zoom out and try to see the larger whole. Look at the organisation, the geographical environment in which the organisation works, look at the branch, its history and the effects that this organisation has on the future world, society and the environment. Look at other things too, even though they are not mentioned here.

- Use your body when reading the text on the website. Where do you notice a reaction to the text? What kind of reaction is it?

- Through this text, what does the organisation include and what does is exclude?

- Which position does the organisation give itself? Which place does the organisation give to the government? Which position does the organisation give to its surroundings?

- What does the organisation say about the balance between giving and receiving on this part of the website?

There are various possible answers to these questions. If you would like to receive feedback about the way you use your systemic wisdom to answer these questions, please send an e-mail to info@systemischwijzer.nl. We will answer your e-mail within a few business days.

If the balance between giving and receiving is tipped it leads to stagnation. You stop actively bringing up good ideas when speaking to your boss, for example. Or you no longer involve your colleague during your professional "cherry picking".The exchange lessens or stops completely. When that happens, the system starts breaking down.

In every relationship there is a "horizontal balance between giving and taking". There is one exception: the relationship between parents and children. In systemic terms this is called the "vertical balance between giving and taking": the parents give and the children take until they have received enough to continue on their own. Children do not have to give back to their parents in equal measure. This would be impossible. How could you repay the ultimate gift you have received from your parents: life itself? Children do not have to even out this uneven balance. The vertical balance between parents and children is a separate discipline and it touches on numerous issues in the area of education, upbringing and even health.

Feeling

3

" *Your body is the best advisor and*
a reliable source of information. "

In the average western upbringing a lot of attention is paid to your intellectual knowledge. The testing culture in schools focuses on children giving the "right" answers to questions such as: *"Why is an energy-saving bulb better than a standard bulb?"* From the age of four, children are tracked using well-developed testing methods. Especially the development of cognitive ability is tested. The observations in regard to emotional development are then added to the report. For example: *"For a five-year-old, Vera is not yet resilient enough. She also does not often play with other children."* When paying attention to the body the main focus is on health in terms of healthy food and exercise. Children are taught that an apple is healthier than a biscuit. Practically every school has a gym where the children can exercise at least once a week. Using your body as an advisor or source of information is a relatively unknown concept in our western culture. If you would like to increase your systemic wisdom you also have to start using your body as a source of information and an advisor. This will provide you with information that is not available elsewhere.

3.1 Your body's wisdom

Knowledge, intelligence and working with your brain are very suitable in certain cases, like doing maths, programming and administering. However, when it comes to evaluating relationships there is a much more suitable source of information: your body. Think back to the last big decision you made. Maybe you quit your job, bought a house or made a large purchase. How did you make the right choice? You probably thought of arguments to underpin your decision and balanced the pros and the cons. When you finally made your decision, where could you feel that? In your stomach? Your heart? Your shoulders? And what did you feel? A cramp? More air? Relieved?

In systemic work you take your body's signals completely seriously.

The information you feel in your body is just as relevant as the information you think of in your mind. From a systemic perspective you look at what is happening in the undercurrent. Symptoms are shown in the overcurrent, the causes can be found in the undercurrent. This undercurrent shows connections, relationships and directions. Information from the undercurrent is easier to pick up with your body than with your mind.

Last year we visited a couple of secondary schools in Amsterdam with our daughter. We had already seen four schools, but she wasn't very enthusiastic yet. She trailed around the schools looking uninterested and reluctantly went to look at the different classrooms. She didn't say a lot afterwards either, she only gave measured answers to our questions about what she thought. The fifth school we went to was the school our son had already attended for the past three years. When she entered the school she was immediately greeted as "the sister of" by several of our son's classmates. She was glowing and skipped from one classroom to the next; happily chatting about how she liked the colours, the children and the school's atmosphere. The cognitive information available on that evening went completely past her, but she had clearly made her choice. Her body language spoke volumes.

LS

For those who are not used to using their body's signals as a source of information it requires a change in attitude. Everyone gets the signals; the only thing you have to do is pay attention to them. This allows you to hear and feel the signals better. You will notice that the palette of signals broadens and deepens when you start to become more experienced. The distinction between the signals will become more subtle.

In the beginning, I always had goose bumps. From one moment to the next I had goose bumps over my entire body. It took a while before it disappeared. It was like an alarm light: on or off. When I started to pay more attention to it and take this information seriously, I became more sensitive to this signal. I no

SB

**longer had goose bumps over my entire body, but only on my
calves, or on my arms. I also felt hot or cold. On my back, in
my neck or in my fingers. It was no longer an alarm light with
only an on/off button; it was now a control panel with lots of
nuances.**

Application 6   *Exercise – Your Body as an Antenna*

This exercise can be done alone or together with someone else. When doing the exercise together you can share experiences. Sharing these experiences out loud will enhance the learning experience.

1. Choose a day with two or three situations that are important to you;
   for example, a day with a presentation, a meeting, or a talk. Make
   sure that you have 15 minutes after each situation to work on this
   exercise.

2. There is no need to act differently during the first important situation. After your presentation, meeting or talk, take the time to look
   back: which signals from your body did you register before, during
   and after the situation? Describe the signals. When doing this exercise together with someone else, tell each other about the signals.
   You do not have to explain them; simply registering the signals is
   enough.

3. When this goes well and you succeed at describing the signals sent
   out by your body, you can continue with step 4. If you are still having difficulties, repeat step 2. Sometimes it takes a while to learn to
   recognise the signals.

4. This step is the same as step 2 with the addition of one question:
   which variables are there? If you start feeling warm, find out if you
   keep feeling warm in the same areas. Also investigate whether it
   happens in the same way (short and intense or more like a wave?)
   and which other signals are sent out by your body. If this is easy and
   you can notice the differences, continue with step 5.

5. Until now you have become conscious of the signals in retrospect.
   This step focuses on paying attention to your body's signals during the presentation, meeting or talk. Just as you know what your

thoughts are, you can register the information given to you by your body. You do not have to do anything with it. There are no right or wrong signals. There is no need to change the signals or make them more or less than they are: you simply have to be conscious of their presence.

After some practice and by repeating the steps, you will start to develop an "on/off button". If you like, you can check your body's signals during an event. That will provide you with more information and it is up to you what you do with this.

The signals that your body gives you generally do not have a fixed meaning. They say something about a specific situation: a relationship, connection or direction. It is sufficient to note the presence of the signal. In the beginning there is no need to explain or interpret it. It can be valuable to say it out loud: *"When you do that, I suddenly feel cold."* The signals often disappear quickly, especially after you realise they are present, but they can recur. You can use them as information.

In my first job as a payroll administrator in a hotel I had to add up the holiday hours of two hundred employees every month. By hand. The number of hours accrued then needed to be calculated pro rata for part-timers. Every month I had a stomach ache during the two days I spent doing this task. The ache was caused by me having to do a task I wasn't suited to at all. I'm simply not accurate enough for this kind of work. There were always angry chefs, waiters and maids standing at my desk to point out the mistakes that I had made. Only when the calculations were automated did the aches disappear.

SB

Using your systemic wisdom and your body starts with including: accepting everything that is present, everything that is possible. Including those things you do not know yet. This is why there is no need to interpret your body's signals. Interpreting them would exclude other possibilities.

Choosing this approach means you no longer work on the "surface" – the overcurrent – but in the deeper layer where patterns develop: the undercurrent. Using your body is a quick and easy way to accept and

connect with everything present, also with the things your mind has not thought of yet.

Application 7   *Exercise – Moving through possible Outcomes*

Think of an actual, current situation in your life. Something that is going on right now, something that is important to you. For example, a decision you are going to make or a relationship that is not going perfectly.

1. Write down three to five possible outcomes of this situation. If it concerns a relationship, an outcome could be *"we would never see each other again"* or *"our friendship would transition into a superficial contact"*. Make the descriptions as powerful as possible. Use a separate piece of paper for each outcome. Make the palette of outcomes as broad as possible.

2. Start with the outcome that is most likely. Say it out loud to yourself or to the person coaching you. Begin with *"I accept that…"*. For example: *"I accept that we will never see each other again."* Say it in such a way that you truly feel it; connect with your heart. Take the time to register how this makes you feel.

3. Move on to the next outcome. Say it out loud again: *"I accept that our friendship will transition into a superficial contact."* Say it and feel the connection with your heart. Notice how it feels different to say this outcome out loud.

4. Continue by doing this with all the outcomes you have written down. Do not work too hard. The only thing necessary to do this properly is the connection with your heart.

5. If you notice that you have difficulties saying an outcome out loud, you can change it. For example: *"I am prepared to find out whether I can accept that we will never see each other again."*

6. When you have examined and accepted all outcomes this way, you will notice that you will move more freely within the situation. There is no longer any fear regarding a certain outcome, nothing has to be hidden. Because everything is allowed to be present, you are free to choose.

There are many ways to work with your body and these are not necessarily systemic. They are not new and have not been discovered by gurus or professors. They are small exercises and simple techniques, which are close to you and will help you to change the situation or the way you look at the situation without too much effort. The exercises will provide information and will complement the other information you have found in other ways.

For me, my body is also a system. The individual parts of my system are not always balanced. I often feel "stuck in my head", trying to approach things in a rational way. At the same time my body gives me plenty of signals. For example, Siets and I had to make the final decision for a Dutch title for this book. After much deliberation, we chose "Systemisch wijzer". We were proud of our title.

LS

Just before the deadline I began to have serious doubts after speaking to a friend who was an expert in management books. He had strong arguments in favour of a different title. I noticed that I didn't really want to listen, but my background in sales made me sensitive to his arguments. So I presented the new title to Siets. She wasn't very enthusiastic, but she was open to professional advice. We discussed the title with our publisher and made a last minute decision to switch titles. Then something strange happened. Instead of being happy with our smart decision, I felt rather sad. I also noticed that I couldn't remember the new title properly. Every time I said it, I said it wrong. These were all signals. I registered them, but did not yet act on them.

During the course of the afternoon I sent Siets a text asking if she had gotten used to the title yet. She hadn't. She had a stomach ache. My shoulders and neck were stiff from the tension. I could barely look at the cover design. At night, hours past the deadline, we sent the publisher an email. In the email, we only described the physical effects of the new title. She understood and respected the message. We were just on time to change the title back again. Goodbye stomach ache. Goodbye sadness. Hello feeling proud!

" *That knot in your stomach is telling you something is not right.* "

Your body reacts to everything happening in your surroundings and in your head. By learning to perceive these signals and use them as information, you can increase your systemic wisdom. Your body does not care for the filters of logic, habits and social pressure. It allows you to literally feel what something means.

SB

The director opened the conversation, "*All right, tell us how things are going according to you.*" My heart started beating wildly and I thought everyone present could hear it. I felt awkward and hot. I wasn't doing very well at that moment. My body was making that very clear. I realised that I didn't want to have this conversation feeling like this. What could help me feel better? This was a rather strange conversation. How strange that the director is asking me this question. It was inappropriate. What is it really all about? My heart rate slowed down. I sat back in my chair, took a sip of water and let out a long breath. I felt ready for the conversation now.

Using your body's signals is only possible if you are indifferent to the outcome and if you are able to accept all possible outcomes. This will hugely increase your range of solutions.

Many of the exercises and techniques in this chapter are used in different approaches, for example in mindfulness and yoga or in dance, music and theatre. Use everything you already know and pair this with the systemic possibilities that arise.

3.2 The empty centre

Using your body's signals as information will increase your reach. The next step towards increasing your systemic wisdom requires that you

accept that everything is possible. This makes new possibilities and solutions visible.

In systemic thinking we call this state of being "the empty centre".
This is the place from which everything is possible and can be examined.
The empty centre might be what is called "enlightenment" in Buddhism.
From a systemic perspective the empty centre is a temporary state of
being that is used as a source for change. Achieving it is not a goal in
itself, nor is it necessary to always stay in the empty centre.

You might recognise the feeling of desperately wanting to perform.
Your heart is beating wildly, you have a stress rash in your neck and your
throat feels like the Sahara desert. If you fail to regulate this stress you
will suffer from a blackout; you do not know where you are or what you
are doing. The opposite of a blackout is working from the empty centre.
The stress turns into a state of peace and confidence. You know where
you are and what you are doing. You feel confident that you are the one
for the job. When looking back, it all passed you by in a daze. That is
how it feels to work from the empty centre.

> **“ When connected with the empty centre, you don't
> have an opinion or plan. ”**

When it comes to the empty centre it is mostly about your intentions.
It is as if you open a pathway to connect with this state of being. Everything that is possible should be allowed to happen. When connected to
the empty centre you do not have an opinion. You have no plans; you internally accept everything that could happen. You do not steer towards
a certain outcome. On the contrary, there is no desired outcome. Your
only intention is to explore and discover what is out there. In accepting
everything, you accept nothing.

The empty centre is a form of surrender: you surrender to what is
happening. Not as a submissive victim, but by transcending yourself
and connecting to the greater whole. That connection – established by
your intention and surrender – shows you new solutions and gives you
strength.

SB Part of my job is to regularly give presentations. Often these are information meetings for groups of employees in which I explain, on behalf of a reorganisation team, what the plans mean for them. My clients are always happy if there is little resistance during such a meeting and not too many difficult questions are asked. I never worry about these things. When preparing for these types of presentations I do two things: I make sure I know exactly what the objective and the contents are. For example, informing staff about a new social plan. I explain how the plan was formed and what the most important points are. Secondly, I connect to the empty centre. I do that by realising clearly that I am only the messenger, the person communicating on behalf of the organisation's system. I consciously know that I don't know everything and that I don't have to know everything. I won't defend or justify anything, but I internally create an open space. In this open space information is shared and the meaning is examined. I accept that everything is alright in advance. Every possible form of anger, confusion, resistance or disappointment, everything is allowed to exist. From this connection with the empty centre I am present and sharing this information. Sometimes it can be hard, for example when I start getting annoyed with someone who is banging on about something. Afterwards I feel tired and dissatisfied. However, when I succeed in passing on the information to the thirty, eighty or hundred and twenty employees and answer their questions from the empty centre, I'm full of energy and new ideas afterwards.

In our society and time we are continuously addressed about what we want to achieve and what we think about certain events. This makes the empty centre a difficult concept. Many things we do start with a wish, something we want. We spend time on it, make a plan and tell others about it. Of course, as a professional, you are not indifferent to whether you get that assignment or not. Working from the empty centre requires confidence: the confidence that every solution is a right solution, over the short or the long term, either for yourself or for the larger system that you are a part of. It also requires courage to accept everything that is possible.

Connecting to the empty centre requires some discipline and surrender. After all, it revolves around your intention. The pure intention to discover whatever emerges, without any goal, fear, or pity and without a specific love for someone or something.

Exercise – Allow everything to be present   *Application 8*

Be completely and unconditionally prepared to allow everything to be present. You are about to carry out seven steps. As you become more experienced it will become easier. If you develop an opinion about the steps – for example "unclear" or "what a hassle" – thank your brain for its opinion. There is no need to do anything else with your opinion yet. Do not ignore it and do not pay any further attention to it. This will allow you to complete the entire journey.

1. Think about all the things that are present in your mind and in your heart. The spinning washing machine. The appointment that you still have to reschedule. The colleague who has made you feel bad. Think about all these things and put them on "standby". They do not have to disappear; you just have to stop paying attention to them for now.

2. If there are any other thoughts making you restless, thank them as if they were people: "*Thank you for making me aware of that. I'm busy at the moment, I'll get back to you later.*" By now you know that, in systems, the things that are not allowed to be seen are exactly the things that appear. By thanking the thoughts and things present, or putting them on standby, you are giving them their own place.

3. Now it is time to internally visit the system you grew up in. Think of your parents and your ancestors. You might feel like smiling at them or giving them a small nod.

4. From this connection with your first system make a brief mental visit to the other systems that play a role in your current life. This can be the system of the family you have established or the organisation where you work. It can also be the neighbourhood or town where you live or the profession you exercise. Once you feel that the most important systems have been addressed, you accept all these systems and do the same with all of the other systems that you have not visited.

5. The next round of visits is to a few abstract concepts, for example: "good and evil", "yesterday, today and tomorrow", "perpetrators and victims". In your mind, you smile or nod at everyone. Everything is allowed to be present, without any goal, fear, or pity and without any specific love.

6. In your mind, visit a place in nature; a place that feels like home. This could be the mountains in Switzerland or the shoreline of the Atlantic Ocean. Find a place that makes you feel comfortable.

7. Finally, focus on your breathing. Consciously breathe in and out. And again. And again.

After following these steps from the beginning right up to step 7 while being connected to yourself, you will be connected to the empty centre. This is a productive place for new ideas, solutions and energy.

3.3 Listening with your entire body

There is a different approach to learning to work from the empty centre: the four different approaches to a situation. Each one of these four approaches is good in its own way and opens the path to new possibilities. This is listening with all your senses, instead of just with your ears.

Downloading

When you are in the "download mode", you look for more of the same. You only accept information that confirms what you already know, information that proves you are right – like a politician who only refers to research that confirms his point of view. You are looking for the recognition and confirmation of your frame of reference and you are not really willing to accept any differences. From a systemic perspective you are simply very loyal to something that is or was important to you. Think of someone who has emigrated. After an emigration the traditions and the culture of the country of origin become much more important.

SB   **I had worked hard to develop a plan for a client. I had followed the rules of the system and involved the right people in the project. Somewhere in the process there was the moment in which**

the picture, the story and the approach were formed. I was happy with it. From that moment onwards I wasn't open to new information. Everything that I saw in the organisation from that moment onwards was a confirmation of what I had developed. I went into the "download mode". I was loyal to my assignment to move forward in the development of this plan.

Open mind

Connecting from an "open mind" means being prepared to change your mind. You do not have to change your mind, but you have to be open to the idea of change. You look at what is new, what is different. You allow yourself to be influenced from the outside and are open to a new perspective or a different view on the matter. You examine the differences but keep to your own point of view and interests. You let go of what does not suit you. For example, in the first phase after a reorganisation you know that the context has changed and that you probably have to change the way you work as well. You let go of the old working methods and examine what is desired in the new situation.

LS

I still clearly remember my first day at the Systemic Work course. Everything was strange to me. It started with having to take off your shoes when entering the room. I didn't understand much of the introduction by the two teachers. They spoke a different language here, a language I didn't recognise. A lot of attention was paid to poetry, stories and art. At the start of every training day a poem was read aloud to establish that day's framework. Initially it didn't have much of an impact on me, but I accepted this new approach. Gradually I got used to it and I started to appreciate it more. I noticed that a poem or story could provide access to another, deeper layer of meaning. In the years that followed I developed my own language for this work. I do remember the poems and stories that were told at the course. I often use these when starting a training or workshop.

Open heart

In the "open heart approach" the boundary between you and the other fades. You might share the same view or swap perspectives; you let go of everything. You can also listen from the heart of the other, with mildness and love, for yourself and for the other. This will open up all kinds of new possibilities.

This is clearly visible in the first stage of a relationship. When you are together, deeply in love, it can be hard to tell where you end and the other begins. You feel fused together. Through that fusion, you discover new parts of yourself. You start liking new things because you experience them from a different viewpoint.

Open heart also means viewing the people with whom you work in the context of a larger whole. That difficult colleague is more than just those opinions and the behaviour that annoys you. That colleague also has an objective and is trying to realise it. Just like you, this colleague has a history and an entire backstory that makes him or her the person he or she is today.

LS

> In the past few years I have attended quite a few amazing pop concerts with my son. If it wasn't for him I would never have thought of going, simply because I wouldn't have known most of the bands. In the weeks leading up to the concert we would practice the songs in the car. Funnily enough we would often have a similar reaction to the exact same part of a song. It was like we had discussed it in advance. During the concerts we often stood there together, simply enjoying ourselves, connected by the music. The boundaries between us disappeared. These are precious memories for both of us.

Open will

Describing "open will" requires abstract terms. You listen from a connection with something larger than yourself and the other. There is more than the sum of everything and everyone present. You listen from the whole, without losing yourself. It is as if everything is present simultaneously. You are connected to yourself, the world around you and to everything that exists, even though you might not know what everything is. You realise that things do not revolve around you.

Barack Obama, the former president of the United States, gives the impression of leading from open will. It seems that he is connected to the greater whole and realises that he is a part of the current times. That he as an individual does not decide what happens, but that he is a representative of something bigger: a temporary guardian of what is already present.

Exercise – Decision making from the empty Centre   *Application 9*

Pick something that plays a role in your life, for example: a difficult appointment or a decision that you have to make.

> *Linda is angry with a manager she works for. She would prefer to stop working on the assignment. She cannot respect someone like that.*

1. Describe several facts of the situation. Describe only the facts and no more than five of them. These five facts represent what this situation means to you. In Linda's case this could be an example of a fact: The manager did not stick to his commitments.

   > *During Linda's holiday the manager sends her an e-mail in which he questions her professionalism. Linda did stick to her commitments.*

2. Consider the situation according to the four different approaches. Start with downloading. Say out loud or write down what is important to you when it comes to this situation: what you want to achieve and why.

   > *To Linda, this situation is about fairness. She is accused of not sticking to her commitments. However, the person making these accusations is the one who did not stick to his commitments: this is unfair. She has made a larger contribution and should be the one to get the reward. The manager is in Linda's way.*

3. If you zoom out a little further, what do you see that you did not see before? Look beyond the situation from an open mind perspective. Perceive everything present as a symptom and know that there are always several ways to look at the truth.

> *It is possible that the manager is aware of something that Linda does not realise. There might be a change elsewhere in the organisation, which has consequences for the project they are working on. It is also possible that Linda is going too fast and the rest of the organisation cannot keep up with her. Or maybe the manager does not understand exactly what Linda is working on and her objectives. In short: there are various matters that could play a role. The manager's e-mail can then be seen as an awkward response to a signal.*

4. Imagine that everything is true at the same time and that everyone is right. It is as if there is a point where everything comes together, without it mattering where it started and who has done or said what. Imagine that this is also true for this specific situation. Where does this open heart approach bring you?

> *Linda realises that she and the manager work for the same organisation. They are part of the same reorganisation process that the organisation is experiencing. She can believe that the manager acts in good conscience and is trying to make the best choices with the knowledge available to him in his position. She realises that the organisation would benefit from her respecting the manager's position and providing him with the right information. This is of more use to the organisation than her avoiding working together with him. It will make them both stronger*

5. Connect to the larger goals you have as a human and the things you would like to achieve in this situation. A doctor might want to make people better and an environmental activist might want to protect the world. Your own larger goal might be closer to home: for example, providing a good income for your family in a job in which you can continue to develop.

6. Once you are connected to these goals and to the here and now, look at the situation again from an open will perspective. Which movement can you identify and what is important?

From this perspective, Linda sees lots of other ways to be of importance. One of these ways is the project she is working on. Moreover, she enjoys the project and she can learn a lot from it, for example, what things are truly important to her and how to deal with "challenging managers".

7. From which way of approaching the situation do you gain the most? Which way will allow you to take a step forwards in this situation? How would you like to move forwards? Carefully consider all four options. Which one suits you best in this context? In the end, the choice in itself is not that important. Considering all four options is a way to connect to the empty centre.

A large part of this book is written from the empty centre. Before I start, I have no idea what I'm going to write. I know what I'd like to write about, I know which message I'd like to bring across, but there is no plan on how to put my ideas into words or which examples I'll use.

SB

I do know how to begin: from the empty centre. I have become clever at connecting to this empty centre. When the concept was new to me, it took a while. I could only connect to it from my own study. Now I can work from any available space, even in a lunchroom where people are enjoying a cup of coffee while they take a break from shopping. Sometimes I find it difficult to write from the empty centre. I might have thought of a beautiful sentence in advance or I might be desperate to use a certain example. When that happens I have a hard time putting the right words on paper. Every noise, every movement distracts me. Later I often don't even understand my own writing.

When I write from the connection with the empty centre it is both a pleasure and it feels like I'm contributing to the world, to the development of this kind of knowledge.

If the empty centre still feels somewhat strange or abstract, allow the concept to slowly sink in. Read this chapter again in a couple of days.

Take the time to explore the concepts and make them your own in a way that suits you.

3.4 Your breathing directs your focus

The quickest way to connect to your body is through your breathing. For nearly your entire life your breathing is unconscious. It just happens. Every now and then you focus on your breathing. In those short moments of conscious breathing there is no other possibility than being connected to yourself, in the here and now. You need these moments to know and feel who you are and what you are capable of.

SB

I was walking through the corridors with my client. We just had a meeting and were on our way to the company restaurant. He was telling me about a difficult situation in the programme he was managing. Meanwhile, we had reached the stairwell and we were walking down. I listened to him and registered what was happening in my own body while listening to him. I noticed that I was restless and my breathing was shallow. In the midst of the grey concrete of the stairwell I interrupted him and said: "*I would like you to breathe deeper. Start by taking three breaths. That's all you have to do.*" It was rather unexpected and inappropriate to say this, but he understood me perfectly. It was as if he was able to reset himself by focusing on his breathing. This provided space.

Breathe consciously. Every type of meditation technique, including modern mindfulness, pays attention to breathing. Breathing techniques are also used by classically schooled musicians and singing coaches. Learning to make public speeches also starts with breathing. The special thing about breathing is that it is a subconscious process in your body, but it can be regulated consciously too. This conscious regulation often does not last very long. It is physically difficult and people often find the experience unpleasant; it can feel as if you are not getting enough oxygen. Even though this conscious breathing only lasts a short while, it has an immediate effect.

Breathing can improve the quality of our connections. Connecting to yourself means being aware of your body and learning to sense and understand our body's signals. Being connected to your body is essential if you want to gain access to your systemic wisdom. Without connecting to your own physiology you only work from your brain. You then use what you know and what you want. This is often valuable, but it is not systemic. You work towards the results instead of towards the source. Breathing consciously immediately connects you to your body.

Your breathing will allow you to gain access to other parts of the body. Focusing on your breathing will allow your brain to get some rest. Paying attention to your breathing opens up space in your mind. You can let go of things. Everything that really matters is strengthened. That space and that strength allow you to carry on.

In the days that followed our unusual conversation in the corridors my client and I made a game of it. When things got tense, or when everything was happening at the same time, we looked at each other and silently told each other to breathe. Later he told me that he had applied the breathing technique to a conflict situation. By not immediately reacting to the other party, but breathing consciously first, he felt stronger. His mind felt clearer. This clear mind allowed him to handle the conflict situation without being overpowered by his emotions.

SB

" *Breathing is the fastest way to the here and now.* **"**

Exercise – Breathing as a Resource   *Application 10*

This exercise consists of three different ways to work with your breathing. Take your time to find out which one works for you and explore the sources you can access by breathing consciously. It is possible that a certain way of breathing will have a different effect than the others. That is fine, this will only increase your choice of resources.

  1. Breathe like you always do. Sit down and close your eyes. Concentrate on your breathing for a minute or two. That's it. Follow

the three stages of your breathing: breathing in, breathing out and the pause in the middle. Let the simplicity of this exercise work its magic.

2. Sit down and place both feet on the ground. You can close your eyes or keep them open, whichever you prefer. Breathe in through your nose, slightly deeper than usual. Breathe towards your stomach – your chest should hardly move. Breathe out slowly through your mouth. Make sure that breathing out takes longer than breathing in. Repeat six to eight times in a row.

3. Stand up and take a few large strides. Move your arms while walking: not very forcefully, but be active. Focus on your breathing. Walk up and down several times.

4. Use the different experiences from this exercise as an anchor. Repeat them so that they become easier. This will enable you to gain access to the resources of your breathing. When you have lost the connection to yourself, choose the type of breathing that can help you best. It is like resetting yourself.

3.5 Slowing down to hurry up

Speeding up is an extremely efficient way to lose the connection to yourself and your surroundings. Slowing down is an excellent way to restore that connection. Focusing on your breathing mainly restores the contact with yourself, your body. Slowing down mainly helps in restoring the contact with your surroundings. You probably know the feeling: a workday consisting of a series of meetings and activities. It feels like being on a train that just keeps hurtling forward. You have not even left the first meeting before starting to think about the second. You feel exhausted and have a hard time concentrating. The easiest way to break this chain is to stop the train. Simply put: everything is equally important, everything has priority.

A rabbi was once asked how he remained so calm
in spite of all his activities.
He said: *"When I stand, I stand.*
When I walk, I walk.

When I sit, I sit.
When I eat, I eat.
When I speak, then I speak."
His audience interrupted him and said:
"So do we. But what else do you do?" And he said again:
"When I stand, I stand.
When I walk, I walk.
When I sit, I sit.
When I eat, I eat.
When I speak, then I speak."
Then they said: *"So do we!"* The rabbi said:
"No… When you sit, you are already standing up.
When you stand up, you are already walking.
When you walk, you are already there."

There are countless simple ways to slow down. In a busy office environment you could switch places. You could take an extra breath before saying something. Postponing a decision, the well-known act of "sleeping on it", is also a way. Try them all and find out what works best for you.

" *Slowing down restores the connection with yourself and your surroundings.* "

Slowing down will allow you to connect with yourself: not only with your head but mainly with your heart and gut feeling.

In my household we start the day at half past seven. My children have to be at school at half past eight. We live within walking distance from the school. Getting up, showering, brushing our teeth, getting dressed, making lunchboxes, eating breakfast, putting on our coats and shoes: on most days everything runs smoothly. The routine provides structure. This structure offers space for unexpected things, such as a glass of milk that gets knocked over, a note that has to be given to teacher or even a quick game of football if the weather allows. The rea-

SB

---

son why I succeed in getting three children to school, washed, dressed and fed, is the fact that we don't rush. We take the time we need for each activity. Sometimes it takes a bit longer; a dress with bow and buttons is more complicated to get into than jeans and a shirt. Then we slow down. Everyone who has kids knows: if you rush them, everything takes longer. Somehow we always seem to have plenty of time. The children help each other make their sandwiches or they eat and make their lunchboxes at the same time. This peace allows the children, and their mother, to start the day in a good way.

Application 11   *Exercise – Managing busy days*

Choose a busy, full day with lots of appointments or different activities. This exercise will slow down your day by consciously starting and concluding each activity.

1. Determine how you are going to conclude an appointment or activity. You can do this by consciously breathing out or staring out of the window for a few seconds.

2. Also determine how you are going to start each activity or appointment. For example, close your eyes for two seconds and bow your head or clap your hands. It has to be a physical action.

3. Start each appointment and activity the way you decided. Also conclude each activity in the determined way. Most importantly: make sure there are a few seconds of nothing between finishing one activity and starting the next. It is essential to maintain a constant connection with yourself.

This exercise will only cost you 30 seconds each time. By making a habit of this you will notice that you feel happier and more satisfied at the end of the day. Slowing down has restored your connection with yourself.

• Do you often play games on your mobile phone when you are waiting somewhere, sitting on the toilet or when you feel like wasting some time? Delete these games. Use these moments to look around you, breathe consciously and simply do nothing for a minute. What makes you feel better?

- Meetings tend to start when everyone has sat down. The chairman clears his throat and opens the meeting. If you happen to be the chairman: wait for a minute or two. Let everyone sit down. Look around you, make eye contact with everyone present and then open the meeting. This also works with presentations, selection interviews and so on. Waiting is an elegant way of providing everyone present with the opportunity to fully take part. It is like inviting everyone's systems to take part in the meeting.

3.6 Your feet know the way

A frequently ignored resource can be found at the bottom of your body: your feet. You can consciously direct your feet. It also works the other way around: you can follow your feet. You then explore the direction in which your body points you. You can literally use your feet to make choices, determine your direction or slow down.

Taking the first step. Step by step. A step in the right direction. Our language contains plenty of expressions referring to our feet. Following your feet means working with your body. Without any intentions, without any goal other than to explore what is there. But how do you do that? Often enough you want to achieve something; you want to achieve a goal. In every form of systemic work it is important that you allow each possibility to be acceptable.

Cheryl was incapable of reaching a decision. Should she accept that new job or should she choose security with her current employer? There are many different ways to approach this question as a coach. Cheryl had already considered all the pros and cons and had spoken to different people about it. So, another conversation didn't seem like the way to go to me.

Instead I asked her to point out two places in the room. The first point would represent her current job, the second the new job. Cheryl had already practised connecting to the empty centre in previous coaching sessions. I asked her to do the same now. From that connection to the empty centre she simply had to follow her feet. Cheryl walked hesitantly and carefully towards

LS

---

the spot she had marked as her current job. When she had almost reached that spot, she changed direction and walked towards the new job, only to return to her current employer. Her indecisiveness was made clear by the movement of her feet. Cheryl literally walked through the thought process that had been keeping her busy during the past few weeks. However, the information she sensed – by letting her feet do the work – was new. She noticed that her feet began to feel unpleasantly heavy when walking towards her current job. She also felt that she became restless and wobbly when standing on the spot of the new job.

Cheryl decided to postpone her decision and to stay put. For the moment. Six months later she did quit her job. The time was ripe for her. Eventually she found a new path in an entirely different position.

Application 12   *Exercise – Following your Feet*

1. Work in an empty area that has a couple square metres of floor space. Choose a project or assignment that you are currently working on or have recently finished.

2. Decide where the starting point is.

3. Illustrate how the project or assignment went by taking steps. Vary between small and large steps, slow and fast, heavy and light, different directions and so on. Take the steps from the connection to your body. Your feet are in charge, they decide how to move. Your head follows your feet. Your feet function as a representative.

4. Do not interpret anything until you have completed your path. Do not think along the lines of: *"I'm taking big steps because this part went well."* Follow your feet and reflect in hindsight, when you are sitting on a chair again. *"What do those big steps mean in regard to the other steps?"*

5. Is the end a point in space or is it more of a direction? Where is it?

6. Have you not yet reached the end point? Then stand on the appointed spot and experience how this feels. How do you view the

path from this end point? Is this spot an end or is it also the start of something new? What is the most logical viewing direction from the end point? What is in front of it and what lies behind it?

7. Choose a small and safe audience for this exercise, for example a peer intervision group or a coaching context. When you become more experienced with the exercise you can also use this technique during presentations or when planning projects.

This exercise is very suitable to test an idea, for example, the planned renovation of your kitchen. After becoming accustomed to this method it is perfectly fine to think of your own variations on the exercise. The way this exercise is set up is only an example.

Exercise – Testing your Planning   *Application 13*

1. Write down each phase of your plans in a few words on a separate sheet of A4 paper. In the case of the example above: *"Choosing colours for the kitchen."*

2. Place all phases that you have written on the sheets of paper on the floor. Place them in an order that seems logical to you.

3. Then literally walk through your planning.

4. Explore your planning with the following questions:
   a) Which steps follow each other in a logical order?
   b) Which step is a condition for a next step?
   c) Which steps should be taken in parallel?
   d) Which steps are close to each other and which steps can be further apart?

   Add any research questions that make sense to you.

5. Adjust the planning using the discoveries made during this exercise. You can also easily test various changes. Which route is easier: choosing the colours first or determining the setup of the kitchen first?

Asking

4

4.1 Systemic questions as a shortcut to the undercurrent

SB

I was telling a colleague and friend how I was doing: how my life as a mother of three children looked like at the moment with a husband who was starting his own company. I told her about my self-employment and how I had to provide an income for the family for the time being. I told her that I was trying to work out several times a week and oh, I was writing a book too. *"For who or what are you working so hard?"*, she asked me. I felt my body react. Everything went silent: from the inside and from the outside. It was as if I could now see the bigger picture. This new image enabled me to make new choices. I'm still just as active, but now I act from an underlying sense of peace that's less volatile, more anchored.

Increased use of your systemic wisdom also means asking different questions. These questions do not focus on a problem or situation. On the contrary, these questions are designed to let your conversation partner zoom out, allowing new possibilities to become visible.

These questions lead someone to a different perspective, a different viewpoint from which to look at the situation. They are questions that guide attention from the overcurrent towards the undercurrent; towards the systemic layer of the life-giving forces. Choosing a good question is one of the most efficient systemic interventions. The quality of the question is much more important than someone's answer. You will notice that introducing a systemic question is often sufficient to make your conversation partner aware of the undercurrent.

LS

I was leading a meeting with a team. The team had only recently been completed. Several sub-departments had been merged and a handful of employees, who had a negative influence on the atmosphere in the department, had been sent on their way. The new manager was also present and wanted to look forwards. At the start of the meeting she shared her vision and future plans with the department. A large part of the group showed an indifferent attitude in a way that said *"we'll believe it when we see it*". Only the two new employees did their best to react enthusiastically. I decided to pay attention to my observation. I asked the question: *"What isn't being discussed here that should be discussed?"* This made a big difference. Employees were – sometimes reluctantly – prepared to join in. A sense of insecurity – *"Who has to leave next?"* – was exposed. We made room for everyone's personal feelings with regard to their colleagues' departure. The employees relaxed. After that the team could look forwards, towards the future.

The questions can focus on a problem (*"How do we solve this?"*), a plan (*"How can we approach this?"*), on an objective (*"How do we reach it?"*) and so on. Sometimes you know or suspect which life-giving force plays a role in a certain situation, but this is not always the case. Often symptoms are caused by different life-giving forces at the same time. These life-giving forces influence each other and interact. A quick, practical answer to a single question does not always do justice to the complexity of a situation. What's more: if the answer is too straightforward, there is a big chance that you are working from the overcurrent. This is of limited value.

If you ask questions in a systemic way, your only intention is to explore. All answers are correct, all answers matter. If your conversation partner does not understand or accept the question, this can be an answer too. What does it mean if the question is not accepted? Is it the question itself or is it something else? To whom or what is this person being loyal by not accepting the question? You can test this by asking a similar question with regard to the same life-giving force. If you suspect that the refusal of the question has something to do with loyalty you can express these thoughts. This can be a good start for the rest of the conversation.

In the organisation where I was working a desirable position became available. I had the best qualifications and the right amount of experience. The management also saw me as the number one candidate.

I looked forward to my new job; in my mind I was already finishing up my current job. However, at the last minute an exter-

LS

nal competitor appeared out of nowhere. I was passed over for the job. I was hugely frustrated and disappointed. Of course I asked my then manager questions to find out on what criteria he had based his decision. I only received evasive and unsatisfactory answers. It also seemed as if he was ashamed of something. I knew that something wasn't right, but I couldn't put my finger on it.

I left the company shortly afterwards. There was no other option for me. Years later I discovered by coincidence that the chosen candidate was a good friend of the manager. The pieces of the puzzle fell into place. At the time I tried to find a rational explanation for my rejection. I ignored the other signals: the feeling that something wasn't right. With my current systemic wisdom I know that avoiding my questions was also an answer. Something had to remain hidden.

" *Your intention makes all the difference.* "

When your only intention is to explore, your question may not contain any hidden feedback, veiled opinions or secret advice. If it does you will notice that you immediately return to the overcurrent. It is like the Wi-Fi signal from the system you were connected with is suddenly broken. Exploring means that you are open to whatever will come, without judgement and without objective. The only goal is the exploration itself. From there onwards you can carry on.

When using questions as a systemic intervention it is important to know from which intention you are asking the question. Your internal attitude, from which you connect and ask questions, makes all the difference. You can compare it to playing a game: are you playing to win or are you playing to have a good time? Your skills, opponents and other conditions remain the same. However, your attitude will decide how you experience the game. This also applies to asking questions. Your internal attitude is more important than what you are asking.

Connecting to your intention happens through your body. So, before starting to work with systemic questions, focus on your body. Do whatever is necessary to achieve an inner attitude of openness and acceptance: an attitude that allows all questions to be asked and all answers to be given. Especially those questions and answers that seem slightly odd at first can provide the most valuable insights.

The better the quality of the connection to yourself, the bigger the possibilities that present themselves in the system with which you are working.

One of my assignments as an interim manager was to ensure that one of the employees would be dismissed. My client told me a long story with various reasons why keeping this person would be unsustainable. Funnily enough I couldn't remember all these reasons or maybe they just seemed unimportant to me the next day. I wasn't sure if I could fulfil this assignment. I decided to examine the situation first.

I arranged to meet the employee as soon as possible. "*There's an odd situation going on*", I said, "*I've been assigned to ensure that you leave this organisation. The reasons why were explained to me, but I keep forgetting them. The assignment feels strange to me. Could you tell me what is going on?*" It wasn't my intention to trap the employee; it was my intention to find out what was happening. The employee started his story. He said something completely different than what I had expected: "*When I was four years old, I got polio.*" Because I had no intentions I could listen to his life story. It took four and a half hours. I was able to listen carefully, without interrupting him. At the end of his story he said: "*Now you know my story and I can leave. All I ask for is a decent severance package and a dignified farewell.*" The admiration my client showed me after solving this case so quickly and cheaply has always been painful for me.

SB

Systemic listening does not add a huge deal to a normal, everyday conversation. It can be helpful in situations in which you suspect that there is more going on – in the undercurrent – than is being told. Not only do you use your hearing, your other senses are also highly active. Systemic listening means watching, feeling and breathing. You withdraw internally and at the same time you are fully present.

The empty centre is the perfect starting point to listen systemically. From the empty centre you open up to all types of communication with the other. Not only through the words used, the intonation or body language, but also in the layers underneath both in intention and in energy. To truly listen systemically it is often not even necessary to hear the words. It is as if you feel the words. Of everything said, what resonates the most? Or is it something that was not said? That can be felt when you are connected to your body. Feeling the words will provide you with even more information.

" Systemic listening is about opening up to the system energy. "

Organisations and other systems have their own system energy. Individuals also have their own energy that can best be described as their personality or character. With some practice it is possible to sense this energy. Systemic listening is about opening up to the energy presented by the other or the situation.

SB At my high school reunion I started a conversation with one of my previous classmates about his work. I only knew him as the impatient troublemaker he was at secondary school. I was curious how this had worked out in his adult life. He told me that he was a manager at a company that invented creative ICT solutions. I could immediately sense how he could be successful as the troublemaker he once was. His system energy had stayed the same, but he had found a constructive way to use it. I left the reunion shortly after this conversation when I started to sense a different system energy: that of my time at high school, where I, as the shy adolescent I was, had felt so insecure.

Opening up to the system energy – and gaining more information in the process – is a start. You consciously open up in order to observe what someone is telling you and how that person is talking. This is especially important during a first meeting. What does this person show? Systemic listening is about paying attention to what someone places in the foreground. What is this person putting in the spotlight?

You then also immediately hear what this person is shoving towards the background. This is a huge source of information – both about the person and about the system – waiting to be tapped into. What is ignored? What has to remain hidden?

A business colleague with whom I had been working for years was going to say farewell. She had contributed a lot to the organisation. As a token of gratitude she was offered a conference and a reception, with the accompanying speeches. My business partner had prepared a very personal speech. She thanked her father – who was amongst the attendees – for all the valuable lessons he had taught her. She said that without him, she wouldn't have made it to where she was now. Everyone loved her speech. At that moment I wondered: what's the matter with her mother?

LS

Exercise – Systemic listening

Application 14

For this exercise, pick a conversation or meeting with an outcome that is not very important. This will make it easier to practice systemic listening without intention or judgement, from the empty centre.

1. The exercise starts as soon as you have finished an activity and you start focusing on the next activity in your diary: a meeting, for example. Focus on the meeting in the same way you have prepared it in your mind. Do not focus on what you want to bring to the meeting. Think of the meeting as a person: someone you do not know yet, who you can observe from a distance, without judgement, with curiosity.

2. Take it a step further. Focus on the meeting from the empty centre.

3. Observe how your body feels. Check your breathing, your heart rate and how warm you feel. Observe how your blood runs through your

veins, how your feet connect to the ground. You do not have to change anything, simply observe.

4. After these preparations, start the meeting. Your thoughts and focus are entirely in the here and now. Switch on or open up all your senses. Once you have done that, take a few steps back. Far away enough to zoom out, close enough to be truly present.

5. Listen with everything you have: your heart, your skin, your history, your knowledge, your eyes, your ears and so on. Also listen to that which is not said.

6. Afterwards, reflect on how it was to listen like this. What did you gain? What did it cost you?

4.2 Universal systemic questions

There are several questions that you can ask in virtually every situation that almost immediately lead to a systemic layer. At the very least they explore what it is that you are dealing with at the moment. A systemic coach or a constellation facilitator will often start with these questions. The questions do not have to be asked out loud. You can also ask them internally, for example when attending a presentation or a meeting in which a decision must be reached. You can stick to the literal phrasing of these questions. You may also think of your own phrasing. Be careful to keep the question neutral, do not use it to point in a certain direction. Keep the question as open as possible.

   Which question is most useful is not always clear beforehand. There is no need to ask every universal question in order to explore a situation. It can happen that one of the questions is so adequate that the other questions do not add anything of importance. Work from the empty centre and follow your instincts.

Universal systemic question 1: Who or what is not seen?

This question refers to the life-giving force of "belonging". The underlying thought is that a system wants to be complete. The question therefore focuses on people, groups, events or parts of the system that are possibly excluded. Use your own intuition when asking this question. What is never talked about, although you would expect it to be discussed?

One of my clients had fully incorporated "appreciative inquiry" in their approach. The method is based on the starting point that you work with what is going well and explore why this is going well. The objective is for you to be able to use the elements discovered in other situations. The method was used throughout the organisation: in assessments, in work meetings, in policy documents et cetera.

In the one and a half years working for this organisation, I had never heard someone say: *"This isn't right. I don't want this."* Rather odd, seeing that there were plenty of issues that the staff were unhappy with. I asked my client why they never said that something simply wasn't good enough or that something had to be better. He didn't understand my question. Apparently, the question wasn't positive enough.

SB

When you are part of the system you are no longer able to see what is not seen. It is as if the system is also hiding it from you. The system requires you to internally leave the system for a short while, for example by zooming out. Or by asking an outsider to point out that what is invisible to you.

Universal systemic question 2: For whom or what is this a good solution?

The current situation is always the best possible answer that can be provided by the system to ensure completeness. The symptoms visible at the surface are actually solutions that the system has come up with in order to complete itself. There is a good reason for the situation being as it is right now. By asking the question this way, you acknowledge the positive intention of the system and those to whom you are posing the question. From that acknowledgement new possibilities arise automatically.

The question *"For whom or what is this a good solution?"* is easy to answer from the empty centre. From here, all potential answers are possible.

The physical responses are often very clear. There is often an initial moment of freezing, holding one's breath or stiffening. *"Oh dear, this is serious."* After that, the person can breathe more easily or start moving.

SB

Parts of this book were written on Sunday morning. A fantastic moment for me to write, but also a moment that is actually reserved for my family. Sometimes I woke up at the crack of dawn, when everyone else was still asleep, and started to write. Sometimes I suggested to my children that they have a "television day" or a Lego party (move the sofas and empty all the Lego boxes on the floor).

I hoped that the children would enjoy playing together or relax during their movie. Sadly, that never happened. They started a row, their drinks fell over, the remote went flying through the room, the one was sitting too close to the other, something broke and so on. Apparently my children are extremely creative when it comes to getting their mother's attention. It was a good solution to the problem of a mother who, at that moment, was prioritising a different system.

Universal systemic question 3: To whom or what does this belong?

Sometimes people take on responsibilities that are not theirs to take. These responsibilities do not match their place or position. They do this subconsciously. By asking to whom this problem belongs, this pattern is made visible. Sometimes the answer to this question is an extensive explanation or a defence why "it is the way it is". That is perfectly legitimate and once again reflects the positive intention of the person and the system. It is the system's attempt to become complete, but not in a way that brings joy and energy. An intervention or a ritual could be relevant in this kind of situation.

Ask your conversation partner whether he or she is internally prepared to return the problem, to bring it back to where it belongs. You can invent a ritual to do this.

Chantal has recently started work at an administrative department. She was introduced by Fred, her manager. They know each other from their former employer, where they happily worked together as direct colleagues for many years. In those days they often had lunch together, during which they obviously discussed what was going on in the department. Now, in her new function within this new organisation, Chantal is a step below Fred in the hierarchy. It takes some getting used to; especially because Fred regularly comes to pick her up, in front of her colleagues, to have lunch. Just like in the past. When they have lunch Chantal picks up all kinds of information that actually isn't meant for her ears; for example, about clashes in the management team of which Fred is a member or about affairs that concern her own department, or one of her direct colleagues. Chantal has mixed feelings about this. On the one hand she's flattered because Fred has confided in her so shortly after joining his team, but on the other hand she feels awkward towards her colleagues. Her "special position" as confidant places her outside the team.

In this example the order is disrupted because Chantal is continuously invited into the domain of the management. She has access to information that does not match her function and to which she cannot react. This results in her not truly belonging to any part of the organisation: not to the management team and not to her hierarchically equal colleagues. The order can be restored once Fred stops sharing information and responsibilities that belong to his own hierarchical layer with her. Or once Chantal sets a limit to the information she receives through Fred.

Exercise – Separating what doesn't belong to you   *Application 15*

Let your conversation partner pick an item to symbolise the task – the problem, the responsibility etc. – that does not belong to him. Ask him to put this symbol down in a spot in a room that represents where the task does belong. A different take on this exercise is that you represent the person or the place to which this task belongs. In that case, stand opposite your conversation partner so he can "return" the symbol to where it belongs. Either way, ask how your partner feels after giving back the symbol.

4.3 Systemic questions from the life-giving forces

Each life-giving force provides different questions. Posing a question from one of the life-giving forces already implies a direction. It can happen that you ask a question from one life-giving force which results in an answer in which a very different life-giving force resounds. In some questions the classification by the different life-giving forces can appear slightly artificial. Depending on the specific situation some questions can also refer to a different life-giving force than the one the question was based on. Posing the question is the start, the opening. That is sufficient.

There is no need to always ask all of the questions. Work with the questions that resonate the most when working with this specific system. In this case resonating means: what you respond or react to. This can be noticed when carefully registering what is happening in your body. Both the pleasant and the unpleasant reactions and signals count.

The questions do not have to follow the literal phrasing: once you become more skilled you can easily make your own variations. It is important that the questions are open and investigative, allowing all possible answers to be given.

Application 16   *Exercise – Understand Life-giving forces*

This is an exercise to deepen your understanding of the three life-giving forces, which also teaches you how to work with the systemic questions.

1. Choose an actual problem from an organisational system, a problem you deal with in your work. This can be an issue in the team you work in or a specialisation you have or that you are aiming for, but it can also be a dilemma about a product or service supplied by your organisation.

2. Write down what the problem is about, according to you, in 150-250 words.

3. Use the questions stated below this exercise. Answer the questions of each life-giving force. Write down the answer or say it out loud. This ensures that you can also feel – with your body – which questions or answers are especially important, instead of just with your head. You will automatically notice what resonates and what does not.

4. Continue zooming out, look out for the next larger whole while keeping the answers to the questions in mind. The further you zoom out, the further you move away from your own reach. In practice only interventions within your own reach can be successful. However, the information from the larger whole can reveal new solutions. See which new, still unexploited possibilities there are to approach the problem.

Life-giving force: belonging

- What is continuously excluded? A variation on this is: what is supposed to remain unseen?

- Who and what belongs to the system?

- What do you have to do to belong to the organisation? A variation on this is: what do you have to do to be excluded?

- What must be given up in order to belong?

Life-giving force: order

- What keeps getting precedence?

- Which order is maintained here and why?

- When was the organisation truly founded?

- What would the founders of this organisation say about the problem?

Life-giving force: exchange

- Who or what gives too much in the organisation?

- Who or what is unable to receive properly?

- How does exchange take place here?

- What is the price that the organisation has to pay in order to change? Who pays this price?

4.4 Systemic questions from various professional perspectives

Most professionals work from a continuous mix of roles and activities in which the required mind-set is constantly shifting. Sometimes the focus is on collaboration; sometimes on leadership, coaching, consulting or being a business owner. In your function there is also an automatic focus on one or several of these roles and activities. For example, as a leader you will inherently have to deal with the term "transference" from your position. Transference can also be part of the other roles and activities. The chosen order is mainly used to illustrate.

4.5 Systemic questions in collaborations

Working together can be fantastic; especially when you get into a flow in which synergy can arise. You then feel like it is possible to achieve everything together. When this flow is lacking and problems arise in a group of people, we often look at the group dynamics first. There has been lots of research into group dynamics and there are many models available in this area. Group dynamics concern the patterns within a group or team and are usually focused inwards. Interventions at a group level, for example bringing these patterns out into the open, can be highly effective. However, you sometimes see that after a while the same patterns return. For someone with knowledge of systemic work this is the signal to look at the problem at system level: not only internally – within the group – but also at the other systems to which this group is connected.

Flow is generated – or hindered – in a team by the exchange between all these different systems. In partnerships, there are always many systems that play a role. Firstly, each individual has his own system of origin, which indirectly plays a role in the partnership. Additionally, there is the organisational system you belong to, the system of your department and the team or product you belong to. Other systems potentially play a role too, for example the system of the professional group you are part of or the system of your client or market. When you cannot solve the problem in a team with an intervention in the group dynamics, it can be worthwhile to zoom out a little further. By widening your perspective, you could possibly see what is going on in the exchange between the team and (one or more of) these larger systems.

Tina was team leader for a team with financial administrative tasks. The team was newly formed after a reorganisation. Before that the staff had worked in other teams, in which they each had a solo function. They knew each other, but hadn't worked together before.Tina was clearly struggling. *"They keep fighting"*, she said. *"One doesn't want to work with another because he doesn't trust the people from that part of the organisation. Another doesn't want to work together with someone who has worked in a team that committed fraud, and then there's one who thinks he's so good that everyone should copy his methods. Where do I start?"*

The first question that you can ask from your systemic wisdom about the example above is: *"For what is the current situation a good solution?"* This question will automatically help you zoom out instead of focusing on the symptoms in the overcurrent: the individual employees who all provide reasons for not working together. Even if you tried to fix all of these individual reasons, nothing would change. Replacing all these employees with new people would not solve the problem either. In this case a more structural solution could be found in the undercurrent, where the life-giving forces of systems apply. In this example we follow the life-giving forces to discover what good reason the system provides for not wanting to work together.

From the life-giving force "belonging" you can ask the question: *"Are there people who are no longer recognised after the reorganisation, who are no longer seen?"* In reorganisations complicated procedures are often designed to form new partnerships. Sometimes these procedures become so complicated that they no longer seem to concern people. Or different measures rapidly follow one another. In that case the strategy often is that any problems resulting from these measures will be solved later. In both situations it happens that people, with their special expertise or experience, are easily forgotten. From the perspective of this life-giving force, the team's resistance to working together is functional. The system is "forced" to show that which is not recognised or seen. This also happens when someone within an organisation is suddenly dismissed or when an organisation harms people or the environment

and then tries to hide it. This can also appear in the overcurrent in the form of a lack of cooperation, as the system's reaction to make visible that which is excluded.

The underlying reason for the lack of cooperation or the resistance can also have something to do with the life-giving force of "order". Not only does everyone who is part of the system have a right to a position; the positions within an organisational system also have a fixed order. Working from this order provides peace and security. Systems thrive on this. In organisations it often happens that people or teams leave their place in the order, then they no longer function from their functional position in the organisational system, with the corresponding responsibilities. Think of an employee in a project team who takes the decisions that should be taken by the project leader. Or consider someone who continuously gives a colleague with the same status instructions and checks their work, but this behaviour is not a two-way street. In both cases someone "places themselves above the other", in a way that does not coincide with their actual position. A different example of "leaving the order" is a manager who by no means directs his team when trying to solve a new problem. In this case he passes off his responsibilities to his team. After a reorganisation – like in Tina's example – it is especially wise to look at this life-giving force. The order has to be "reinvented".

There are also good reasons not to work together stemming from the life-giving force "exchange". After a reorganisation the organisation has to "reset". The dust has to settle. In terms of the time this takes, the guideline is one cycle, for example one financial year or a term of election. Everyone has to reconnect to the system. The order has to be re-established. This requires extra energy from the staff, whereas it is still unclear what they will receive in return. For that reason, a reorganisation disturbs the balance between giving and taking in the undercurrent. It is possible that someone appears to gain a lot in the overcurrent, for example by getting more opportunities to develop, better working conditions or working closer to home.

When there is a new reorganisation within the period of the first cycle this introduces an extra risk factor. Employees are busy connecting to the new situation, which costs extra energy, and then are forced to let go again. It can then become less and less interesting for someone to connect to the organisation or to the goal of the reorganisation. They have already given too much. Just when they get to the point of receiving something in return for their efforts, they have to give again. Moreover, what and when they can expect something in return is uncertain, which disrupts the balance even more.

The exchange and balance between giving and taking can also be disrupted in teams that have nothing to do with the consequences of a reorganisation. For example when the production requirements are constantly increased without there being any kind of reward. Or when staff competencies and qualities that were previously highly appreciated by the organisation are suddenly of lesser importance.

Tina immediately knew why the staff was restless. " *The management kept saying how important the reorganisation was, how much better everything was going to be, and that everything would be much more efficient. It was as if we had never done anything right in the past, when I think that the staff had actually managed quite well with the few resources available. They had prevented disasters.***" When we looked past the boundaries of the team, we saw that lack of acknowledgement was actually a problem in the entire organisation. It manifested in several different forms. In systemic words: there were a huge variety of symptoms. Tina got to work with her own team. She organised a team meeting about lack of acknowledgement and the balance between giving and taking. Together we approached the management and planned a meeting about the symptoms that we had noticed. The management reached the same conclusion as Tina and changed its communication strategy. The first concrete step by all members of the board was to visit the teams and hear what was lost during the reorganisation. All's well that ends well? Not quite yet. However, making a start by bringing up the undercurrent gave the management a better grip and more possibilities to successfully lead the new organisation.**

Questions about working together

- What is the lack of partnership really about? Does the symptom belong to one of the people in the team? Does it belong to the entire team or to a part of it? Does it belong to a larger system?

- If the behaviour of a certain person bothers you, ask yourself what function this person fulfils for the system by showing this behaviour. Is he ensuring that someone or something is not forgotten? Is she safeguarding quality?

- How come you are the person looking at this situation? Whose role or what need are you fulfilling for the system when you do this?

Accept all possibilities as hypotheses when answering these questions. Imagine that the lack of partnership is indeed due to a person, what does that mean? What does it say? Imagine that the lack of partnership is indeed due to a team or a part of a team, what does that mean? What does it say?

Work with the above questions with the intention that everything is fine the way it is. Nothing has to change. The actual situation within the team or within the organisation is the system's best solution for the time being. Acknowledging this gives the symptom a function. This is exactly the right function for the symptom. This gives it a fitting place within the system and allows you to continue your work. The symptom shows you the direction in which to start exploring. Going over the three life-giving forces – like we did in the example – can provide the necessary structure for this exploration.

Systemic questions for leaders

From a systemic perspective, leadership mainly concerns the questions about order. Being a leader means something along the lines of "taking up the first position". You are hierarchically placed above a group of employees. The tasks of the highest placed leader within an organisation (director/CEO) are as follows:

- Guiding the organisation in its exchange with its surroundings (the market, the company's physical surroundings and so on). An organisation that does not contribute to the outside world has no reason to exist.

- Setting limits: indicating the norms and behavioural rules. What is wrong and what is right within this organisation? This shows what the organisation stands for and makes this clear to all the people who belong to the organisational system and all the parties that exchange with the system (such as clients, suppliers and other stakeholders).

- Creating a safe context, in which the employees can take their positions (with the accompanying tasks and responsibilities) and use their potential to contribute to the direction and objectives of the organisation.

When a leader does not completely fulfil his leadership role you often see someone in the hierarchical level underneath (or even lower) step forward to take the position. This instantly causes turbulence in the organisation's undercurrent: the order is disturbed.

Questions about leadership

- From which internal position are you acting as a leader? Who or what are you trying to be for the people you are leading?

- What do you need to accept leadership from others? Do you recognise this from your family of origin?

- When you make a decision, from where do you make it? To what or whom are you connected? What or whom are you serving? Which system are you working for?

From a systemic perspective, leadership gives you a higher position in the organisation's order. The leader's position can be compared to that of a parent in the family system. The employee's position in the organisational system can be compared to that of a child in the family system. The same dynamics are at work in the undercurrent. Because of this it often happens (subconsciously) that an employee looks at the leader and recognises one of his parents. The result then is that the employee starts acting from the dynamics of a child towards his parents. As a leader you will always encounter this "confusion of roles" in your staff. This confusion of roles is called "transference". Transference is the repetition of an older relationship in the here and now. In this transference, all kinds of old feelings and expectations, which actually belong to the parents, are projected onto the leader. Every leader or manager encounters staff transference in his position.

SB

Richard is a department manager and manages eight team leaders. During a meeting with me he is interrupted. One of the team leaders, Otto, sticks his head around the corner and proudly informs us of how he handled a workplace situation. There was no urgency whatsoever and the problem had been solved. When the team leader is gone, Richard looks at me with raised eyebrows and apologises for the interruption. "*When he sees you, he sees his father*", I say. "*He looks to you for the acknowledgement he would have wanted to receive from his father.*" We looked at each other and we both knew it was true. "*Now I know how to approach him*", said Richard.

We are all familiar with the normal, daily transference. Think of the obviousness of you being a student of a school, partner in a relationship or parent of your children. That transference is, in most cases, extremely functional. Without having to think about it, you know what is expected of you in these relationships, what "playing field" there is and what is possible. This makes life comprehensible. There is no need to think about everything: some things you just do. You know that if things work out this way, you can achieve your goals.

As a leader you inherently deal with transference because a hierarchically higher position easily evokes transference. Recognising and pointing it out is often sufficient to stop this transference (by the employee). There are three ways to identify transference. Firstly there is an exaggerated emotional reaction. An employee reacts more strongly to you than what is appropriate in the situation. Secondly, you can recognise transference by childish behaviour. You will then see that the employee is no longer able to react in a mature way or that he or she is performing below his or her ability. This is called regressive behaviour, like in the example of Richard and the team leader. Thirdly, you can recognise transference by a pattern of circular behaviour: when communicating to the employee, it feels like you are going around in circles. It is like a record that keeps getting stuck in the same groove.

There are three ways to deal with transference. In the example with Richard these are the options:

1. Richard can accept the transference by giving Otto what he is asking for: acknowledgement and recognition. This can be effective in the short term, for example during a starting period, in order to make someone feel at home. In the long term this does not contribute to someone's autonomy and development.

2. Richard can also choose to refuse the transference. In that case he ignores Otto's (subconscious) call and makes it very clear that he is not Otto's father. He might not use those literal words but he can mention the pattern to Otto. Without making any value judgement, he can tell Otto what his behaviour brings to mind. Otto is then made aware of his pattern. This can ensure an atmosphere of openness in which to discuss mutual expectations and responsibilities.

3. A third possibility is to undermine the transference by giving the opposite reaction of what is requested. He can do this by ignoring Otto or listening without much interest. The objective here is to make him think and contribute to his autonomy. When choosing this option it is a good idea for Richard to explain his actions at a well-chosen moment. After all, it is not his objective to continuously undermine Otto.

Questions to explore transference towards you as a leader

1. Which forms of transference do you regularly have to deal with as a leader?

2. Which form of transference do you often evoke in staff? Is this connected to your position as a leader or manager or do you also encounter this outside of your work?

In addition to transference there is another specific issue that applies to the principal leader of an organisation: there are no direct equals or colleagues, you are alone. There are no "brothers or sisters" to share with. As the primary leader of an organisation you have to be able to deal with the loneliness that comes with this position. Being able to handle this verticality requires that the top leader deals with "not belonging to the group". Leaders who do want to be part of the team disrupt the order. Just like parents who want to be friends with their children. It does not work. Children then lose their parents, employees then lose their leader.

One of the most destructive acts a leader can perform is saying: *"I'm one of you, we're equal."* This is not true. The message in the undercurrent towards the staff is then: *"There is no leader here. There is no guidance, no limitation and no security."* It would be preferable for a leader to say: *"We are part of the same system. From my position, I will do the best I can to serve the whole as well as possible."*

LS

In an organisation with only flexible workspaces, the director Leo has his own office. He has lots of meetings, mostly confidential, and he needs time to focus on his work without being distracted. Leo had been criticised for not being visible. This left him wondering whether he should give up his own, fixed workplace and start working in the open-plan office.

***"Make sure that you are available without sitting in the open-plan office"*, I advised him. *"Your special position involves a different kind of work. Sitting in the open-plan office like everybody else wouldn't be a smart move. You're not equal to your staff."* Leo was clearly surprised. *"Be available by having lunch with the others every now and then, and clear some space in your schedule to answer your team's questions and listen to what they're doing."* Nothing changed psychically. In the overcurrent, everything stayed as it was. However, for Leo, a lot had changed. He now works from a different internal position. That gave him and his team peace.**

Questions about fitting in as a leader

- How do you as a leader or manager deal with verticality and "not being part of the team"? Or what do you observe in the leader(s) of the organisation(s) for which you work?

- Which position feels easier or more familiar for you personally: the leadership position or the membership position? How does this reflect your role in your family of origin?

These questions are meant to help you reflect. Answering them will help you explore your own patterns. Which position in the group has become "normal" for you and do you naturally take? Often this is the same place you take in the first system: your family of origin. Insight into your own patterns is the first step towards learning to move more freely between membership and leadership.

Systemic questions for consultants

When two people meet there is more than just these two people. The systems behind these two people also meet. Each one of us has our own system of origin, the family in which each of us has grown up. However, there are also the systems of your professions, the system of the role in which you meet, and the systems of your organisation(s) that play a role in the conversation. This applies to advisors, but also to trainers, interim managers or contractors in any form. You are loyal to each of these systems in a different way. These loyalties influence the possibilities and sometimes even decide them. These loyalties virtually always play a role and are extra clear when it concerns a contractor. This is due to the relationship between a client and a contractor. The contractor is autonomous and has knowledge that the client does not have. He decides what to do within the context of the issue posed by the client, but the client is the one who finally decides whether to implement the contractor's answer.

All kinds of systems play a role when a client chooses and assesses the contractor. To find out which system and which loyalties play a role when giving advice about the assignment, it is valuable to be aware of three different "places". These places are the magical place, the assigned place and the serving place.

In your youth, which formed you into who you are today, you learned all types of patterns. These patterns are natural to you and result from your system of origin. You might have learned to take care of others. In your adult life caring for others then usually becomes a place that you easily take, both automatically and also in the assignments that cross your path.

SB

In the summer holidays my sisters and I always went to the pool. The three of us used to bicycle across a four-kilometre dike to get there. As the oldest, my task was to get everyone to and from the pool safely. I made sure the pool memberships didn't get lost and sometimes we would get some money to buy ice cream. I would be the one to look after the money.

As an adult woman, taking or having responsibility is perfectly natural for me. I never lose my keys. I always know where my wallet is. I always make sure that I can look after myself and others.

It's no different in the workplace. When someone asks me to do something, I either accept or refuse the task. If I accept the task I give it a hundred percent. I do whatever is necessary to finish the task even when it goes beyond what's stipulated in the agreements, for example if it takes longer. I don't bill those extra hours. I take that responsibility.

In systemic terms, the place that is closely connected to your family of origin and the place where you feel comfortable is called the "magical place". In the example above it is "taking responsibility". The term "magical" is used because it originates from the illusion that a child can fix whatever is lacking within the family. Children will do everything to get love, attention and security. They are sensitive to what is lacking in a family and will fulfil that part. You grow up with certain behaviour, which feels safe and normal. The behaviour and movements that you make from the magical place feel familiar. You have developed strong behavioural patterns from here. When you behave according to these patterns you feel loyal to the group conscience of your family of origin. You feel comfortable and "innocent" when you act from the magical place. Everyone has these behavioural patterns. They are neither positive nor negative. They are simply there.

LS

As a child I did well at school and I had a talent for volleyball. I grew up with mottos like "never give up" and "always finish what you started". This was natural to me. I was an easy child.

My parents never had to urge me to do my homework, I was always well prepared for volleyball practice and even found the time to play, read or do something creative. My independence was increased when I was selected for the Dutch Junior Team when I was fifteen. From then on I often went off on my own for training trips or international volleyball tournaments. I loved the space and independence! I still enjoy organising my own life. My willpower and ability to begin without being prompted are strong impulses – from the magical place – that I easily engage.

Because you have spent a large part of your life in the magical place you are very familiar with it. This behaviour is so familiar that it remains easy to engage in as you mature. You have developed lots of your qualities from this place.

In systemic theory, the position offered to you by the client is called the "assigned place". The assigned place is the task formulated by the client. In the overcurrent this concerns the results that are expected of you as a contractor. In the undercurrent – sometimes subconsciously or unspoken – it also concerns the role you are expected to fulfil. People are highly sensitive and clients are usually perfectly fine-tuned to what you can contribute to the organisation or team. Therefore you are generally asked and invited to act from your magical place. Job applicants are also subconsciously selected on this basis.

In the assigned place the risk is in the "outsourced assignment". The client then tries to outsource (a part of) his own tasks and responsibilities to you, consciously or not. Something that belongs to the client and the organisation system is then handed over to you. In the undercurrent of the assignment there is an invitation to fulfil something for the organisational system from your position of contractor.

I had accepted an assignment as an external strategic advisor, for eight months. I had to write and implement labour market policies to ensure a better market position for the organisation. Subconsciously – for me and for my client – this assignment called upon my sense of responsibility. The responsibility for this strategic policy was outsourced to me.

SB

Any policy I could have come up with would never have worked. Whichever way the organisation might turn, they were the ones responsible for their own strategic policy. Not me.

In many cases it is fine to work from your magical place. Also when it coincides with the assigned place offered by your client. You are in your element and the assignment makes the most of several of your qualities. Still, the magical place is not always the place that serves the organisation of the contractor most. Especially when you sense that there is an outsourced job in the undercurrent of the assigned place, it can be useful to contract in a pure way.

In your role as a contractor you can avoid accepting an assignment with an outsourced job. This is achieved by seeing the assigned place – the tasks as originally formulated – as an opening bid and not as an accomplished fact. It is the starting point from which you will explore what is going on in both the overcurrent and the undercurrent, together. The assigned place is nothing more than a framework from where the contracting can begin.

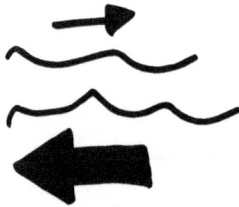

A client is often perfectly aware of your qualities. Indeed, you were probably approached because of these competencies. However, accepting the assigned place does not automatically mean that you serve the organisation in the best possible way. Working from the "serving place" often means doing something different than what you were first asked to do as a contractor. In the serving place, you not only intervene in the issue's overcurrent but also in the undercurrent. Drawing attention to the undercurrent is obviously much more challenging than just doing your job. There is a risk of not getting the assignment, especially if the client does not want to look at the undercurrent or act upon it. In the serving place you respond to the client's issue from a different place and perspective. Obviously your responses do fit in with the original request, but you broaden the "playing field" of that request. This is achieved by posing questions and providing answers that lead to the undercurrent. This reframes the issue.

The difference between the magical and the serving place can be noticed through your options. In the magical place, the options are limited. You act the same way you have always done, from loyalty to your family system. In the serving place you do something different, something that might even go against the group conscience. This makes you feel guilty, but also shows you that there are many more options. This is the result of literally being less "bound" to your system of origin in the serving place. From here you can tap into the organisation's growth potential much more effectively.

LS

My client Jan, for whom I have been providing sales trainings for some years now, asked me to join him at a sales meeting in Denmark. As soon as I had heard the word "Denmark" I had already enthusiastically responded "yes". I had no idea what I'd be doing there or what was expected of me. It turned out that the team would receive a product training and that I would have to translate it into a sales pitch. The assigned place. I found it strange that Jan wanted to invest so much money and valuable time in this project. When I was informed about the reason for the international trip, it became apparent that something else was going on.

The sales manager, who previously managed the team, had been placed back into the team by Jan. There had recently been more turnover and discontent in the team. Jan wanted to solve this with this trip, as a kind of incentive. Jan reckoned it would be good for team spirit and motivation.

I noticed that I felt sceptical about this. I didn't think that the discontent in the undercurrent could be solved with a fun trip. I said that I only wanted to join as a team coach, not as a sales trainer. Jan accepted this change in the assignment. Together we designed a programme and clarified our roles. The serving place was found and appointed. It was an unforgettable trip.

When you notice that an assignment is becoming a struggle without there being any identifiable substantive reason, examine from which place you are working as a contractor. It might be necessary to cancel the agreements and negotiate a new contract. This is not an easy solution, especially not when you are in a financially dependent position. However, from your systemic wisdom this is the only right choice.

Questions for the contractor

- What are you connected to most in this assignment? Does this connection belong to the assigned place, the magical or the serving place?

- Under which conditions can you make a different choice?

- Who are you, as an advisor, for this system?

Questions for the client

- From which system and which loyalty did the offered assignment arise? Which other systems also play a role? How are the needs of these systems pictured?

- Who has decided what the advisor is working on now? Who made the actual decision?

When you accept an assignment from your systemic wisdom you not only work with the part of the organisation that hired you but with the whole organisational system. You continuously look for ways to strengthen the whole. The assignment's meaning in the systemic context therefore differs from its analytical context: the assignment formulated from the client's position is always a symptom of something larger. Contractors using their systemic wisdom do not have to make themselves appear larger than they are. They work from the awareness that what people see is always part of a larger whole.

Systemic questions for coaches

As a coach (or in a coaching role) it is important to be aware of your intentions. The role of coach already implies that you are going to help others from that role. Many coaches took up the profession because they like to help others and love contributing to their clients. They are fully dedicated to using their coaching skills and life experience to help their clients find themselves, become stronger or develop their talents, all with the very best intentions. Coaching from your systemic wisdom requires you to examine your intentions, especially if you want to help. Because, what kind of help really helps? From a systemic perspective the coach places herself above the client when she (subconsciously) presumes that the client needs her help to get any further. However, the effect is then completely the opposite: coaching from this intention makes the client smaller. It deprives the client of his autonomy because it – ever so subtly – puts him in a position of dependence. This is not immediately noticeable in the coaching relationship. In the overcurrent the client will show joy or relief and he will be thankful for the steps that will be undertaken in the coaching sessions. But what happens in the undercurrent? What does it do to the client's autonomy as a colleague in a team or as an employee within an organisation?

It can happen that a coach is subconsciously trying to restore a balance between giving and taking. The coach feels compelled – once again subconsciously – to give something back to others because she has received a lot in the past. This often happens with coaches who have received lots of help, for example when recovering from a burnout or with a new step in their career. This can trigger a natural need to give back. Many coaches once chose the profession because of their own positive experiences with coaching. They have gained so much from it in their personal and professional life that they now wish to pass on these insights to others. This is an effect of the life-giving force "exchange".

The "helper's syndrome" is not foreign to many coaches. However, helping from the position of a parent immediately invokes the child position for a client. It deprives the client of his autonomy. On an underlying level you could even say the coach maintains the coaching relationship because the coach benefits from it. Coaching fulfils her own need to give. The coaching relationship then turns into a therapeutic relationship that, in theory, could continue forever. Using your systemic wisdom starts by looking yourself in the mirror: do you dare ask yourself from which intention you are truly coaching? For whom or what are you working? What are you "restoring"? These are certainly not easy questions to answer. The ultimate question to find out where you stand is: *"Am I here for the client or is the client actually here for me on another level because I want or need something?"*

Start with acknowledging the situation as it is. Being aware of the fact that you may be restoring a balance as a coach already makes you freer of it.

Sometimes it is the other way around. Clients can also be needy. In that case they call out to you as a coach: *"Tell me how to do it, I can't do it myself"*. They address the coach like a child addressing a father or mother. This can happen very explicitly, for example when a client asks you which choice you would make in his place or when the client requires constant reassurance or approval. Moving to the position of the child also happens implicitly, without words. You then often see someone suddenly appearing much younger, either in terms of facial expression or manner of speaking. In these cases the true need of your client, in the undercurrent, concerns the parents. In that moment you, as a coach, are seen as a surrogate parent. If you do not watch out, you will fully take part in the transference: before you know it you will answer to the client's need – with good intentions – from the parent position.

It's easy to fall into this trap, especially if you are a coach with a strong desire to help others.

Questions to ask as a coach

- When asking/saying this, how old are you? Asking a client's age will make him aware from where he is responding. He can then consciously choose how to carry on.

- If you want to achieve this goal, to whom or what must you be disloyal? This question stems from the strong loyalties that can be felt towards parents.

- At this very moment, what strengthens you most of all? This question increases the client's autonomy.

It can also happen that a client has a clear objective in the coaching. He wants to achieve something and only looks to the future, to the profits. How great it will be if he learns this one thing... When a client has already tried to achieve this objective in various ways, these questions are powerful. They show the client that it is also possible that something in the past can obstruct the way forwards. The client can then sense the limitations imposed by his loyalty towards the family of origin, especially when it comes to themes such as daring to "fully aim for success" or "fully choose your happiness". It is as if you suddenly make the elastic band – which keeps pulling someone back to the child position – visible. This awareness can make all the difference.

Edith would love to start her own company as a trainer/coach. She successfully completed a course as a trainer and found a fitting name for her company. Her business cards and website are nearly finished. Now that the moment approaches to actually launch her own business, it stagnates. Edith indicates that she is usually very business-like and decisive, but that she now has lots of doubts. This confuses her. When asked "*To whom are you disloyal when you take this step?*", she immediately answers: "*To my father.*" Her father is a successful businessman in the car trade. He does not understand that Edith is giving up her career as an account manager to take up something as

---

"soft" as training and coaching. Edith now realises that she is subconsciously waiting for her father's approval. She lets out a deep sigh and looks up. *"I now know what to do"*, she says.

The client is most powerful when connected to the here and now, connected to the person he is right now, including all the experiences and capabilities he has gained in life. Systemic coaching also means that, as a coach, you trust that every client can carry his or her own fate. This attitude prevents you from trying to ease the client's circumstances, carrying his fate with him or taking up a parent position. Accepting the client and his system of origin – everything included – is the only right starting point from a systemic perspective. You can adopt this attitude by envisioning the client's entire family system. You not only see your client, but also his family of origin, up to three or four previous generations. This helps you zoom out. Your attention and empathy not only go out to the client, but to the client's entire system. Adopt a friendly, mild view. You do not have to know the names or know what they look like. Imagining them is sufficient.

Application 17   *Exercise – From Child to Adult Position*

If you notice that a client tends to take up the child position, you can use the following exercise. This exercise helps the client reconnect to his adult side and thus strengthen his autonomy.

1. Ask the client to close his eyes. Check if he is sitting comfortably and feeling connected to his body.

2. Let the client look at his parents in his mind. His father first, then his mother.

3. You are a coach, not a therapist. Limit yourself to the here and now. If the client becomes emotional, ask him to calmly keep breathing.

4. In the original exercise the parents are the source. However, you can translate the parents into the professional surroundings. Who or what is the professional equivalent of the father and the mother? It can be a product, a manager or a customer group. The essence is that the client accepts a source bigger than himself. Ask the client to first look at his father and then at his mother. He does not have to do anything else.

5. As a coach you give your client's parents a place in your heart. You acknowledge them as your client's parents and respect the past, whatever has happened, without judgement.

6. When you notice that the client feels satisfied (pay attention to their breathing, a sigh is always a good sign), invite him to conclude in a fitting way. This can be a nod of the head, a sigh; there are various options, as long as it does not require too many words.

During the first coaching conversation with a new client he made a casual comment about not being happy about his weight. I considered that casual remark as one of the coaching questions and mapped out the route after the first conversation, in which losing weight was one of the goals. In the following conversations he did not want to discuss weight loss strategies. After a while he confessed that my enthusiasm to incorporate it in the coaching programme had a reverse effect. He felt that it was my goal instead of his. Saying this out loud gave room. I realised that I had projected my own standard, from my own system, on him. On the other hand my client realised that he had been exposed to a repeat of messages he had heard in his youth and he realised how he reacted to this. It was the only way he had been taught to react as a child: to sulk and block all communication.

Our family systems had their own place in this coaching relationship. By engaging my own family system (in my mind) I could maintain a mild attitude towards myself and avoid passing judgement over my behaviour. In a way I could feel my ancestors behind me. The coaching programme has been completed. In the meantime, my client has dropped twenty kilograms and is extremely proud, because he achieved this at his own pace using his own choice of resources.

LS

Questions for the coach

- Who or what am I as a coach for this client?

- Who do I first accept in my heart: the client or the client's system?

- Which transference – from you as a coach – lurks here?

Accepting the client's system, without wanting to add or change anything, is a good starting point for a fruitful coaching relationship. Accepting your own system of origin, without wanting to add or change anything, is a requirement to stay clear of transference.

Systemic questions for business owners

This just might be the most personal part of this book. We are both are entrepreneurs. This is not self-evident.

Entrepreneurship, from a systemic perspective, means starting something new and transforming something that exists and bearing the risks and responsibilities that accompany this. Being a director in paid employment or an employee who receives shares are, systemically seen, not versions of entrepreneurship. A director who does not function well is dismissed. He receives a different place in the system or disappears entirely. If an entrepreneur does not do well, the whole system disappears.

Being self-employed means dealing with many systems to which you are loyal or disloyal. The views and moral attitude towards entrepreneurship in your family of origin play a big role in this. Think of your family. Who would support you as an entrepreneur? Who would not? Were you raised to choose certainty? Or to choose new options and take risks? Ask yourself: *"From what intention have I become an entrepreneur?"*

SB I had a job that would make plenty of people jealous: enough opportunities to develop, a good salary and close enough to cycle to work. I was heavily pregnant and in the middle of a major home renovation when I quit my job. It was a considered choice and my husband fully supported me. Without knowing what would follow my maternity leave. The only thing I knew

was that I couldn't carry on like this. I felt trapped in my job
and I couldn't grow. The question that kept playing through
the back of my mind was: *"How long are you going to keep this
up?"* My entrepreneurship developed from my desire for freedom. The price, uncertainty, is one I was more than prepared
to pay.

Although there has been little structural research into the matter, it
seems that business owners who are focused on exchange are the most
successful. They contribute to other, bigger systems. In other words:
business owners who mainly focus on their own interests are less successful from a systemic perspective. They may be successful when it
comes to making money, but then pay the price when it comes to health
or their personal life. It seems as if there is some kind of "universal balance". This balance surpasses the boundaries of money, taxes, time and
the ego. From the perspective of the life-giving force "exchange" a company that is solely founded to earn money cannot be sustainably successful. The same goes for products or partnerships. There has to be
a healthy exchange with the surroundings for there to be a true reason
for existence. Money earned at the expense of the environment or the
vulnerable groups in society seems to flow away from the person who
receives it just as easily. Money, health or energy: systemically speaking
these are different manifestations of the same flow of exchange with the
surroundings, focused on a healthy balance between giving and taking.

During my first phase of self-employment I did everything I
thought was necessary. I had set targets for myself: every week
I had to have two appointments with people who could possibly contribute to my business. I had to make the most of every
networking event that presented itself. Business cards? Check!
Elevator pitch? Check! Smart yet stylish appearance? Check!
I felt truly unhappy during that period of time. I came to take
something and felt like there was nothing I could give in return.
All these appointments came to nothing despite my hard work.
I started a partnership with people with whom I felt no real connection, simply because I didn't want to miss the opportunity.

Only when I allowed myself to say *"no"* to certain appointments

SB

did I start to get a better sense of who I was as an entrepreneur and what I had to offer. From then on the opportunities came rolling in. Now, years later, I feel as though there are opportunities everywhere. I know who I am, what I'm capable of and where my boundaries are. Those boundaries have strengthened my entrepreneurship.

LS   I often notice that entrepreneurs struggle with their company's identity. Who are they and what is their product or service? Clients or customers expect a strong, clear story. I too struggled with this when I started my own company as a trainer /coach. It was quite easy for me to arrange meetings with potential clients. So far so good. However, when they asked me what exactly it was that I did, I had no clear answer. It was because I did all sorts of things. I sensed that most clients weren't looking for that answer. Also, "all sorts of things" didn't give me satisfaction. It was time to bring order to my service range.

I already did a lot of storytelling in organisations and now it was time to apply this powerful method to my own company. My storytelling partner guided me through the different steps. She was the "critical conscience" that ensured that I didn't lapse into wishful thinking and catch-all terms. I discovered my leading principles as an entrepreneur: what is the core of my business and who am I for the people that come across my company? This immediately led to more focus in my service range, a new company name and (finally) a website, in which my identity was visible and tangible. Writing this book – almost three years later – seemed to be the next step. The exchange with the outside world has been in full swing ever since. An increasing number of doors open from the inside.

Thanks to the life-giving forces we know that a connection to the surroundings and a healthy exchange with the outside world are essential. That can be quite challenging, for example when a company has already existed for several generations. Sometimes you see the third or fourth generation continuing the company in the exact same way as it was handed over by the parents because this feels safe. The company was successful this way and it seems most respectful to the parents and the former generations. Seen from a systemic perspective they are acting out of loyalty towards their parents, while risking stagnation of the exchange and the company going out of business. A more free form of this loyalty can be achieved by transforming important parts into the present. For example by taking the most important values from the past and translating these to the current company. Acknowledging that "the way it used to be" was fitting in the past and acknowledging that the times have now changed will both be beneficial to a healthy exchange.

Isaac is a third generation bulb grower. Together with his girlfriend and their three children he lives in the house where he grew up. Isaac took over the company from his father when he was thirty. Before that he completed several courses of study, travelled and worked in an entirely different sector. Not long after taking over the company he transformed it to meet to the demands of today. Large sheds were built and the production process was completely upgraded.

It is now up to him to keep the company healthy, make enough money from it to provide for his family and prepare for the moment when one of his children has finished studying and travelling. It is likely that by then he will walk across the yard every now and then, just like his father does now, and give advice that belongs to a different era.

Asking questions and entrepreneurship

- When are you an entrepreneur? What makes you an entrepreneur? Are you successful as an entrepreneur and how do you know this?

- To whom or what are you loyal or disloyal by becoming or being an entrepreneur? Who or what decides whether your business may be successful?

- What price do you pay for your entrepreneurship?

- Where is the real difference made?

- Whom or what does your business really serve?

Sometimes entrepreneurs lose themselves in continuously trying to improve their product or service. *"If I knew even more or supplied even better quality, then…"* It then seems like the entrepreneur has lost the connection with the outside world and is unable to see the larger whole. The quality of the improvement is often not visible or tangible for the end user. It is interesting to then examine which good reason the entrepreneur has to not be truly successful.

Doing

5

SB   It has already been several years since I was introduced to systemic work and started to try and develop my own systemic wisdom. I was continuously looking for something to hold on to. Give me instructions so I can follow them, I often thought. Tell me what to do. Only seldom did I receive instructions I could actually work with …

In this chapter we describe several applications. These are all examples of working methods that you can try in order to extend your systemic wisdom and enjoy good results. Becoming systemically wiser means working in the undercurrent, using your body's signals and working with the whole. An exercise, intervention or question can only be systemic when you are connected to the system with which you are working. You can also apply the described working methods without working systemically. It is possible to intervene in the overcurrent; however, this usually makes no difference to what is happing in the undercurrent.

Making more use of your systemic wisdom in any case means connecting to the system.One way to achieve this is working from the empty centre. This means that you are free of judgement and do not steer towards any desired or undesired result. You internally accept that all outcomes are possible. In addition you activate your entire body – your own system. To achieve this you not only use your cognitive intelligence, you consciously register all the signals your body provides and take them into account. Verbal or written instruction is not needed. It is all about how you organise yourself.

The described applications and working methods can be seen as guidelines. You can apply them literally, just as they are described here. You may also add your own ideas. Feel free to use all your experience and knowledge. Sometimes, during an exercise, you might get an idea for a variation on the working method. Examine where this idea is coming from. The empty centre is a reliable source. Does the idea originate from your connection with the empty centre? In that case it is usually advisable to follow your idea. Sometimes an idea originates from your own discomfort or insecurity. In that case, head back to an area that makes you feel comfortable and secure. Choose a known and familiar working method. Although you are not working systemically, it does allow you to work on "your own system" when you reflect later. What happened? What would help you? After all, all possibilities are present simultaneously. Systemic work is not an end in itself.

5.1 Working with lines

Suitable for

- Everything that can be approached in a linear way, for example time

- Opposites: yes/no, satisfied/dissatisfied

- When order plays a role: time, yes/no, 1-2-3-4-…10.

There was a meeting planned for 150 members of staff at the municipality where I was working as an organisation consultant. The objective was to inform the staff about the course of a radical change process that would be finished in six months. The changes were going to have a substantial personal and professional impact on the staff. It had been decided that each project leader had to inform the staff about the state of affairs of their own project in this change process.

Before they started I used masking tape to draw a long line straight through the room where the staff was already waiting. One end represented the starting point; the other end represented the end date, six months later. I made the project leaders' boss take a place at this end too. I instructed the project leaders to follow their feet and stand on the place that represented where their project was now. Afterwards, every project leader was allowed to briefly explain their position. The mutual relationships and dependencies were immediately visible.

The combination of a visible timeline and the project leaders' explanations had a strong impact. Not only did the staff listen to all of the presentations with more interest, there was also more understanding and clarity, and it took less time.

SB

Description

Decide on a point A and a point B. Decide what the points or the line represents. Choose a place on the line.

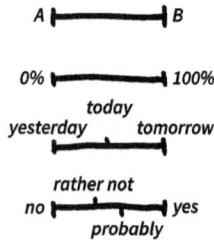

Variations

A ├────────┤ B

0% ├────────┤ 100%
today
yesterday   tomorrow

rather not
no ├────────┤ yes
probably

- Let people examine several places. For example, if your line represents progress – like in the example above – let people first choose a place that represents "now".

  - How does it feel to stand there?

  - To what is your attention drawn?

  - Who is enjoying the current place? Who is not?

- Ask everyone to look back to where they came from. Let them connect to this place and they might even walk back towards it. *"Oh, that was how things were when we started."* This can be especially useful when several people were not present at the start as it will allow them to establish a better connection.

- Then return to the place that represents the current situation. Ask whether something has changed after standing here the first time. Are things better or worse? In what way?

- Before asking the next question, ensure that people are truly connected to their bodies. You can draw extra attention to it, for example by saying: *"Feel how you are standing here. Feel where your feet are, how they feel. Notice the way you carry your shoulders. You don't have to change anything, simply observe.*
Be aware of the temperature of your hands, your head and your feet."

- Then invite them to walk towards the end point. Observe how they do this. Big steps? Hesitantly? State what you have observed. You do not have to give any meaning to it: the only person who can do that is the person who made the movement.

- You can conclude the exercise by walking back to the place that represents the present. Ask whether anyone would like to say anything.

- Add a point C as a possibility that also exists, but was not visible before. In the example of the meeting this could represent a point where one project flows into another, or where the assignment is changed in such a way that the original project is transformed. Do not be too specific about what point C could mean. Pay attention to the question whether point C should even be allowed to exist. Are all possibilities acknowledged? Observe who pays attention to point C. What does that person represent? Then continue by removing point C. How have things changed compared to the beginning, when point C was not there?

- A simple way of working with lines is the "line-up". In this exercise you let a large group of people stand in order based on a certain criterion, such as age, seniority (who has been working here the longest?), years of experience in a certain field et cetera. You apply an explicit order. This form is particularly suitable as a fast introduction exercise. This does not make it systemic. Generally the energy is too high for that. It is possible to intervene, for example by outlining a certain context that everyone deals with in their work. If you then let several people switch positions – for example the boss and an inexperienced employee – a number of people will not only know, but also feel that "something is not right". The undercurrent is now activated.

Points of focus

- Sometimes people take the place of "the right answer" or stand in the socially desirable spot. When you suspect that this might happen or notice this during the exercise, you can add the following exercise: "Stand in the desirable place" or "Take your place on the spot where you think you should stand". After that you ask the person to go to the place that his or her feet know is the right spot.

- Be very careful when defining point A and point B. This decides what the exercise is about. For example, if you want to find out how happy people truly are about a situation you will get an entirely different response if point A is a 0 and point B a 10 then if point A represents "dissatisfied" and point B "satisfied". You can always ask the people you are working with (the participants) what the right definition for A and B is.

- In dilemmas it always seems to be about choice 1 or choice 2. However, sometimes there is no logical connection between choice 1 and 2: there is no line and they are two unfixed points. In that case you can use the

"quadrilemma" working method.

5.2 The quadrilemma

Suitable for

- Examining a dilemma or issue

- Reaching a decision

- Gaining insight and information about various potential solutions.

LS

Jack has successfully been working in organisations as an interim advisor for years. He is usually hired to analyse and improve business processes, often projects that take six months or longer. He recently finished a training and coaching course. Jack also enjoys working with the people in organisations, maybe even more than taking care of processes. He is now struggling between changing direction and continuing his old job. In a coaching session I choose to work with the quadrilemma. I pick four chairs and place them in a diamond shape with four equal sides.

The first chair represents his role as an advisor. The opposite chair represents his role as trainer/coach. These two options represent the classic dilemma. The third chair represents the option "both", the fourth "neither". I let Jack take his place on all four chairs and tell me what he feels in his body. I consciously don't ask him what he thinks; he's rational enough as it is... He only sits on the "neither" chair very briefly. It is immediately clear that this is not an option for him. He tries the other chairs a few times. *"The trainer/coach chairs feels most comfortable"*, he says. However, his body language is unsettled and seems inconsistent with his words. Jack looks solemn and

---

seems wobbly. I decide to test something and remove the "advisor" chair. *"Well"*, I say. Jack looks surprised and begins to laugh out loud. *"No, this isn't right at all"*, he says. We put the advisor chair back and Jack tests the "both" option again. Now he suddenly feels comfortable in this chair; he happily settles into it. Almost immediately he comes up with an idea about how to apply his newly acquired expertise as a trainer/coach to his current interim job.

Description

A quadrilemma is a variation of the dilemma in which you examine two alternatives that are both equally (un)attractive. The quadrilemma is a simple working method that follows a fixed structure. Together with the person who contributed the dilemma, you examine not two, but four potential alternatives.

1. Take four empty sheets of paper (A4 or bigger) that will represent the four positions of the quadrilemma.

2. Use a marker to clearly indicate the four positions: A is "the one", B "the other", C "both" and D "none of them". A and B together are the existing dilemma, C and D are the new possibilities.

3. Place the sheets on the floor in two straight lines that cross: place A across from B and C across from D.

4. Let the person contributing the dilemma say it out loud. Make sure that the dilemma is clear so that everybody present is aware of the two options that make up the dilemma.

5. Ask the person contributing the dilemma to stand on sheet A and decide which of the two options it represents. Then let the person stand on sheet B and say out loud which alternative this sheet represents. Do the same with the other two positions, C and D. Observe what happens to the person contributing the dilemma in the different positions. Pay attention to your own feelings and thoughts as a coach.

6. Examine the "circle" of the quadrilemma again. Ask the person contributing the dilemma to consciously connect to his body. It

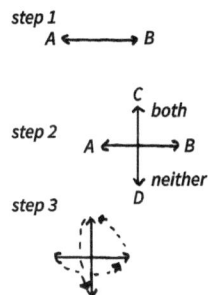

might be easier if he closes his eyes first. Ask questions such as: *"What do you experience in this position? What are your bodily sensations? What do these tell you? In which position do you feel more comfortable or calm?What makes you enthusiastic? What doesn't?"* As a coach, do not be tempted to rationalise or interpret. If you notice this happening, zoom out a little further; simply observe and register what is happening.

7. Pay attention to any physical changes when the subject stands in the different positions. Think of posture, way of moving, firmness, breathing, facial expressions et cetera.

8. Allow the subject to repeat certain positions as often as he wants in order to test what they feel like. Does it strengthen or weaken the subject to stand in a certain position or move towards it? Where does the subject feel this in his body?

9. Do not be afraid to try things, such as removing options that have been rejected. Keep looking at the effect on the subject and examine together whether there is a solution available.

Variations

You can swap the sheets of paper with all kinds of other objects, such as chairs, slippers or cushions. It does not matter, as long as you stick to the structure of this constellation.

- Doing this exercise with a group, with four people representing the four positions, will supply you with extra information. This way A, B, C and D can also relay information, from their position and their observations. Choose whether or not to work with other people based on the phase of the subject's decision process. Also observe the extent to which you as a coach are familiar with this method. If the subject is still immersed in his internal decision process, it might not be desirable to involve external eyes and ears.

- For advanced coaches! If the subject still has no idea what direction to choose or decision to make after a few "circles" within the quadrilemma, it can be interesting to add the so-called "free element". This stands for "none of these and neither that" and thus represents a lot more than just a fifth alternative. Preferably choose a person to represent this free element, simply because this will help you gain more information. In contrast to the four fixed positions in the quadrilemma the free element may do anything that occurs to him or her. Sometimes it is not immediately clear what this fifth element stands for. This does not matter. The most important thing is that you take the information gained from it seriously. The penny will drop later.

Points of focus

- Keep checking whether you are approaching the quadrilemma systemically or rationally as a coach. Pay attention to whether you are connected to the empty centre and if your body is switched on as a source of information. If this is not the case, slow down. Quietly walk through the quadrilemma with the subject and feel, see, check and know what is happening to you.

- If the subject walks in a certain direction, ask where this movement stems from. Is he following his free will? Is he doing what he usually does? Or is he pulled towards something? Whatever the answer to these questions, it does not matter. It is all about the meaning the subject gives to it.

- You can also start with five elements straight away. In that case you can introduce the fifth element straight after examining the four positions for the first time.

5.3 The organisation chart

Suitable for

- All questions in which the order is unclear and/or parts are potentially excluded.

- A good start of an intake interview during a training, coaching or change process.

When I start a new assignment I always want to know how things work in this system. Sometimes I stay in the background   **SB**

until I have worked things out, sometimes I specifically ask my client. I don't ask for the formal hierarchical order as this is usually well structured. I ask how things function in everyday situations. During a new assignment, focusing on improving customer orientation, I asked the director to draw the organisation chart. I noticed that he did not include the customers and didn't even mention them! His entire focus was directed inwards. Customer orientation had become the politically correct term that everyone in the organisation was talking about, but the customers weren't noticing any differences. When the director gave the customer a place in the system during an experiment, he realised what he had to do. From then on he considered customers as part of his company and knew what he had to work towards in order to give the term customer orientation a true meaning.

Description

1. The coach draws the positions of various people, functions and groups in relation to each other, as in an organisation chart. The best way to do this is by asking the people who know the situation well. The coach may be anyone, as long as he or she is not part of the system that is being examined. As a member of a system it is often logical for things to be the way they are; loyalty to and involvement in the system can make certain issues invisible. It is easier to make certain connections from outside of the system. In the following explanations A is the person talking about the organisation chart and B is the outsider: the coach or the person asking questions.

2. B asks A the questions below and incorporates the answers in the organisation chart. B draws the answers exactly as she hears them. The result rarely resembles the formal, hierarchical organisation chart. That is because you are working with systemic reality.

3. Before you start, decide why you are doing this. Use the questions below, or a variation on them, to draw the organisation chart.

manager of
my manager
sales
department
me   *my*
       manager
large customers

- With which system are we going to work?

- Who belongs to this system?

- Who else?

- Where do you position yourself? Has that always been your position?

- Which special events have occurred?

- Where is the pressure? For whom or where is the going tough? Who is carrying too much or a burden not meant for them? (question for the coach: from which loyalty?)

- What was here first? Give that its own place in the organisation chart.

- Who or what is not seen?

- What has not been said yet?

Variations

- After B has drawn the organisation chart, you can vary by using objects to represent the most important positions. These can be coffee cups, teabags or post-its, but you can also use other items. By moving the items around you can now try out different options. Focus on the options that you can influence yourself. For example, change the distance between your function as a team leader and the other teams or add something to the organisation chart that previously was not present – in the latter case think of clients, products, events from the past or former colleagues.

- From question 3 onwards every question is an opportunity to delve into a new topic. Ask yourself whether asking such questions suits the role you represent in this organisational system. Sometimes there is space for a coaching approach, sometimes there is not.This depends on your tasks and responsibilities. From a systemic perspective, when you go beyond the agreements made you are making yourself larger and the other smaller.

Points of focus

- In this exercise it can happen that A says something along the lines of: "*No, that's not right. It should be like this.*" As B, it is important to maintain a firm connection to yourself, the empty centre and the system. Check whether the quality of the connection is strong enough: what does your body say? Is it "on"? In that case there is a connection. If that is not the case you are working in the overcurrent and so is A. It is then likely that you are focusing on the contents or on procedures. This is fine in itself, but very different to systemic work, in which you work with the patterns and dynamics in the undercurrent.

- Make sure you do not incorporate too many of your own experiences or interpretations. Well known variations are: "*Yes, I recognise that*", "*Shouldn't... actually be...?*" and "*That seems difficult*". Incorporating your own experiences or interpretations will make you zoom in whereas this exercise is most effective when you both zoom out and create order.

5.4 Table constellations

Suitable for

- One-to-one conversations

- It is an effective way to get a problem or situation "out of your head". By making a three-dimensional representation you can reach a diagnosis or solution.

LS I regularly use table constellations during my coaching sessions. Sometimes with dolls or coloured chips, but often I simply use things that are already on the table. I was in a coaching session with Rachid, a young manager who had just started as a department leader for three operational departments. At that time, they hadn't yet found a replacement for his previous function as head of the service department. So, for the time being, he had kept that position too. During the session it soon became clear to me that Rachid was passionate and had difficulties setting boundaries. When I questioned him about

---

this, I noticed that he tended to downplay things. It wasn't that big of a deal, he said. I asked him to place all of his current tasks on the table. Before long the entire table was full of salt and pepper shakers, glasses, tea lights, coasters and cups. Only when Rachid included an item to represent himself did he realise how much he was doing and how alone he was in his tasks. After that we examined and tested all kinds of possible positions and interventions. The table constellation was an eye opener for Rachid. He decided to establish his boundaries and ask for help. Meanwhile someone else has taken up his previous position and he is getting better at delegating tasks. He now turns to his own manager more often for back up and as a sparring partner.

Description

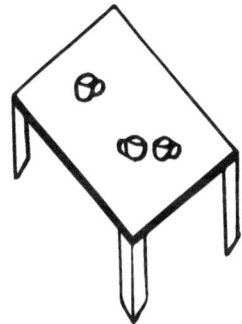

1. Choose materials that are suitable to use during a table constellation. These can be dolls (for example Playmobil people), shells or other small items.

2. The subject decides which elements are relevant to his issue. Do not be tempted to use too many. Try to use a maximum of seven elements to avoid cluttering. "Less is more" is the phrase to go by! Only use more elements if that is functional, like in the example above. Additionally it can be enlightening to see someone having to choose which elements to incorporate in the first place.

3. Ask the subject to quietly put all elements in their place. The issue and its context are now represented on the table. You can now both look at and experience the complete picture as outsiders. The subject's internal picture is now made explicitly visible. This usually provides mental space and peace, which enables the development of new possibilities.

4. Allow the subject to experiment with several positions, for example by increasing the distance, turning things or adding an element. Continuously look and feel what effect this has on the total picture and on the separate elements. Leave it to the subject to give meaning to this. Ask questions such as: *"Have things im-*

proved or worsened for you?", "What could be a first step towards realising this situation?" or "For whom or what is this the ideal outcome?".

5. The length of this exercise can vary. Sometimes it only takes a few minutes for the subject to become aware of what is happening or what the next step is. Sometimes it takes longer. In any case, stop if you become aware of trying to turn it into a "pretty picture" or when the subject takes on a "yes, but" attitude. Also stop if you become aware of your body signalling that it is time to finish up.

6. The subject decides how to continue. Would he like to let the image of the constellation sink in? Would he like to take a picture of the constellation? Would he like to continue with the next step straight away? It is often helpful to not immediately discuss the constellation with the subject but to let it rest.

Variations

- A table constellation can also function as a starting point. You start working with small items on a table. Then you continue in a larger space, using cones (from the gym) or coloured mats as representatives.

- Make a constellation representing the subject's desired final result, knowing that this (still) differs from reality. At the start of every session, check whether this picture is still correct. If not, what is different about the currently desired final picture?

Points of focus

- Many small items are suitable, but some items are easier to work with. Firstly, it is much clearer if the differences between the elements are visible. Be sure to pick items that have a front and a back; this allows you to determine the "viewing direction" of the element. There are also ready-made sets of figures available that have been specially designed for table constellations. Do an online search for "figurine sets for systemic constellation work".

- As a coach, be aware that you keep working in a systemic way: in the undercurrent. Do not incorporate too many of your own experiences or opinions. Zoom out further if you notice that you are getting stuck in your own thoughts or assumptions. Assume that everything is possible. Pay attention to the subject's response when something is changed within the playing field. Tell them what you observe, without passing judgement.

5.5 Resources

Suitable for

- Extra support during slightly stressful situations.

Like every self-employed person I now and then have an interview with a potential client. I used to get rather nervous about these interviews. For example, because I really wanted the assignment or because I felt intimidated by my conversation partner. There is one conversation that I will always remember. I was terribly nervous and was desperate to get the job, but there was a lot of competition. Whilst waiting my turn I saw the competitors: two men in smart, slim-fitting suits. They looked impressively professional. I noticed that I felt intimidated, small and ignorant: not a good internal attitude to start an interview with. In my head I had already lost the assignment before even introducing myself. A few moments later they came to collect me. I decided to not bother telling them how professional, smart and so on I was. There was no way I could beat my competitors ... "*I'll just show them who I am and that's that*", I thought. In record time, we started swapping ideas, opinions, visions, ambitions and a lot more. The energy was electric. Forty-five minutes later all four of us were exhausted by the intensity of our conversation. When I left, I saw the two men again, waiting their turn. You might as well go home, I thought to myself. This job has already been assigned. It didn't take long before I got the call. It was the beginning of a long-term cooperation. This experience has become a resource. Now, when I feel nervous about an interview, I connect to the way I felt before and after that specific conversation. My slightly unsympathetic thought still makes me chuckle a bit. This resource helps

SB

me go into these interviews feeling relaxed and confident.

LS I'm a member of a group of systemic professionals that organises monthly family and organisational constellations for business clients.   Through this group I have been able to coach many clients over the past years. This has given a huge boost to my development and confidence as a constellator. I have experienced how important it is to have a support system, especially in situations in which I was nervous. I tend to do things on my own, purely on willpower or from some kind of urge to prove myself. This is not always a good attitude, especially not in the field of family and organisational constellations. In this constellation group I learnt that "doing things yourself" is entirely different to "doing things alone". The group has become a true resource for me. I regularly use this resource before and during a constellation. I visualise "my group" standing behind me, giving me encouraging looks. In that moment I sense that I am part of a larger whole and that I am not alone. This helps prevent me going into "overdrive" when things get confusing or I get nervous. This also helps me to stay close to myself.

5.6 Description

Visualise always having something or someone with you to support you to give you the courage or strength that you lack. Or to point out the humour of a situation, so you can continue feeling relaxed. We call these things or people resources. You can create your own resources using virtually anything. These can be people surrounding you, functioning as a role model, inspirer or pillar for example. But also negative experiences: the "never again" notion as well as nature, animals or art. In essence, you connect to the resource that specifically strengthens you in the area where you need it. This exercise mainly concerns mental reinforcement. This is achieved as follows:

1. Decide when and for what reason you need a resource. Be as specific as possible: "*Next Tuesday I have to give a presentation to the management team. I know what I'm talking about, but all those managers looking at me make me insecure. I'm afraid they'll ask questions I don't know the answer to. I want to feel confident, so that I can provide a professional contribution.*"

2. Decide what is needed. In the example: what is needed to feel confident? This can be anything: humour, creativity, indifference, playfulness and so on. There does not necessarily have to be a direct link between the two. There is no direct link between confidence and playfulness, but if access to your own playfulness helps you feel more confident it is a good idea to start with this playfulness.

3. Provide a word or form for the resource. This should be something that you can connect with and that functions as an entrance to the resource. It can be a word that sounds pleasing to you. For some people playfulness is a word that provides energy, for others it may be associated with childishness, which means it is not the right word. You can also pick an object as a symbol.

4. You now turn the object or word into a resource. This can be achieved by connecting to it in your mind. You can say it out loud or in your head: "*This ring is now my resource. Each time I connect to this ring I will feel more confident.*" Another way to do it is to welcome the resource: "*It's great that this ring helps me feel more confident. I am thankful for this and will use it respectfully.*"

5. The more attention you give to a resource, the more powerful it becomes. Take the experience with you in your mind for a few days and think about how you want to use the resource. Ask yourself how you could use the resource in the current situation. In a way, it is like you are befriending the resource. You could write something about it or choose an object to symbolise this new resource and keep it close.

Variations

- Instead of words or objects you can also choose people to act as a resource, like in Leanne's example. The person or group of your choice does not have to be aware of this: you simply use your own projection. It also does not mean that you wish you were this person, that you always like this person or agree with all their actions.

- Instead of starting from a need – you would like to feel confident – you can also start from an experience. An inspiring conversation, for example. Or a touching movie you saw. Or last week's frustrated feeling that you had because no one was listening to you. You can decide to turn that experience into a resource. Frustration is often an excellent resource for courage. A touching movie can reconnect you to your underlying values. An inspiring conversation can quickly be turned into a source of energy.

Points of focus

- It is not necessary to always have resources for every situation. You can turn everything into a resource. Choose two or three that can help you at the stage of your life you are in now. After a while you will not need them anymore, which means you can replace them with other resources.

- You can give the resources their own place in the room you are in: place an object on your desk or adjust your screensaver. You can also carry your resources with you, for example in the form of jewellery or as a note in your wallet. The resources can also exist in your memory or imagination, for example a deceased grandparent or the archetypal mother. Give these a place too. According to the order of constellations the place on your left-hand side is intended for someone who (or something) who supports you. This is generally a good place for a resource. The leading position is on your right-hand side. This is not an ideal place for a resource, because you want to maintain the leading position yourself. Behind you is the place for everything and everyone you originate from. This is also a good place for resources, especially for family members, mentors or precious memories. In general it is a bad idea to place a resource in front of you because it becomes too dominant or will maybe even block your way. Somewhere in the distance, but within your vision, can be suitable. Experiment by visualising which place ensures the most strengthening effect for the resource.

5.7 Testing

Suitable for

- Individual decision-making. You have to choose between several options.

SB This exercise is often used when there are choices that have to do with work. This was the case with Susan's question. The company she worked for had offered her a promotion. Susan hadn't been counting on this. Without her colleagues knowing, she had applied to a different employer and she had got the job. At the same time her brother, who owned a thriving company, asked her to work for him. That was how, all of a sudden, Susan had to choose between three different jobs. She found this extremely difficult.

We placed four chairs in the room. One represented the promotion, one the external job, the third stood for working for her brother's company and the fourth represented all the other possibilities. I did not tell Susan which chair represented what. In a sense it was a "blind constellation".

I instructed Susan to first examine the chairs: walk around them, look at them from a distance, and maybe touch them. The only thing she couldn't do was sit on them. All she had to do was be aware of her bodily sensations. Susan walked around intently and described her feelings. The amount of choices paralysed her; she felt lost. Looking at the choices from a distance made her feel stronger.

From this position she chose a chair to sit on, simply in order to become conscious of her physical reaction. After sitting for long enough, she went back to the place where she felt strong. From this position she chose another chair to sit on. We repeated this until she had had enough. One of the chairs was by far her favourite. *"This is how I want to feel"*, said Susan. *"Exactly like this."* The easy option was to now say what this chair represented: *"There, another case solved."* However, it was more powerful to work with the different sensations Susan had experienced. She now had a reference framework on

how she should feel in the place that suited her best. This enabled her to more easily talk about her choice and thus reach a decision that fitted her.

Description

The example above more or less describes how to systemically give shape to a test. As a coach you ensure neutrality, you include all possibilities and you help the other to stay connected to his or her body. Also remain aware of what every change does to your own body. Turn the chairs into representatives by touching the chairs and saying in your mind: *"This chair represents…"*. Try to keep your descriptions as short and factual as possible.

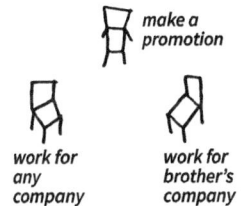

make a promotion

work for any company

work for brother's company

Variations

- A smaller version, derived from working with chairs, is the use of items. Choose small items from your surroundings that can be held in your hand, for example a pen, telephone or glass. Decide what each item represents. Do not associate too much: this excludes too many options. Hold the item in your hand and connect to it. How does it feel to connect with this and thus with this option? Also see the points of focus below for this version.

- Let the person testing the chairs give each chair a defining term. This does not necessarily have to be a specific bodily sensation. The word should reflect the essence of that spot, for example "exciting" or "unsettled". Those words can be used as input for following conversations or coaching.

Points of focus

- This method is demanding. The first requirement is that each participant is genuinely and fully prepared to face all possible outcomes. If you sense that this is not the case, this is fine. Acknowledging this is also a form of taking a step forwards. If not all possibilities are allowed to be fully present, the exercise becomes one on a more rational level.

- The second requirement is that the participants have to trust the method. For someone who is used to making decisions through logic and argumentation this method is very much in contrast to their normal approach. If you notice any resistance to this method, do not use it. Or try the exercise anyway and decide that there is the possibility that you will be surprised.

- Limit the number of options that you want to examine to a maximum of four. If there are more options it is advisable to first investigate these in another way, for example with a table constellation or with an organisation chart.

5.8 Systemic intervision

Suitable for

- Experienced intervision groups and intervision groups with a coach.

LS In the networks that I'm part of, intervision is a much-used learning method. I often notice that the members of a group start to get slightly bored of each other after five or six sessions: by then they know each other well. In one of those groups I suggested performing the intervision in a systemic way. We used other questions, connected differently in advance and promised not to work too hard or help each other. Even before we started a lot had happened: it was a new beginning. The agreements about not working too hard and not helping each other gave the intervision the new purpose. With a small ritual – everyone stepped over a line drawn on the ground with masking tape to represent the step from the old to the new intervision form – we bid farewell to the old purpose.

After this first time we started every following intervision meeting with the questions: "*To which purpose are you connected by being here?*" This question helps create the field from which we could work together, without having to desperately hold on to each other, the form, or the old agreements.

Description

1. Begin with a silence. Slow down. Make sure that everyone has the opportunity to let go of everything that might be going through their minds. Invite everyone into the here and now to take part in the intervision with everything they have, with everything they are, were and can become.

2. The group can choose the person introducing the case in advance. It is also possible to allow the process to take place more organically: the group then agrees to be prepared to discover what the meeting will be about this time, without making any decisions beforehand. This second method can only be used when the participants have enough experience with self-reflection. In this case it can be more powerful to let the system of the intervision group decide the programme instead of the individuals. The further explanation is based on an individual introducing a case.

3. Spend about five minutes discovering the case. The person introducing the case could tell something about it, the others can ask questions. By no means are any solutions provided. The aim is to examine and deepen the case the group is dealing with. An exact description is not necessary. Invite the person introducing the case to think out loud, explain any self-proclaimed dilemma and so on. All questions, all reactions are meant to keep the field around these questions open. Everything has to be able to flow.

4. In the first round the others explain what they physically felt during the introduction of the case. This is solely about bodily sensations. *"When you explained… I got goose bumps."* Or: *"I heard you say… and my heart rate increased."* No further explanation is needed. Do not expect everyone to feel the same sensations, simply share yours. The person introducing the case is silent and listens. He or she might want to thank the others with a small nod or a short *"thank you"*.

5. In the second round the participants can examine which systems are playing a role. It might also be possible to order the systems. *"I keep hearing the loyalty towards the system in the case. I recognise the subject's question, we've discussed something similar before. I think this question is actually the organisation's question, more so than the subject's question. Because it's so well-known it's not that strange that he's the one asking this."*

6. In a third round there is space to freely philosophise about the question: *"For which problem is the current situation a good solution?"* The person introducing the case reacts by only describing his bodily sensations.

7. In the fourth round the question *"What have we not yet seen?"* can be examined.

8. The intervision is concluded by thanking the person introducing the case. Allow this person to dream, ponder, fantasise and forget. Do not give any advice, not even in a disguised form! Do not ask for a first step either. The systemic intervision is part of a process. The exchange and the flow of the process are interrupted by advice and agreements. You would then be asking for a commitment to something that is not yet finished.

Variations

- In chapter 3 systemic listening is described in the forms "downloading", "open mind", "open heart" and "open will". Agree with the participants who will listen in which form.

- You can plan a moment of silence between each round. Each participant connects to the way in which he or she is present. Which system, which intention was dominant? Wait until after the intervision before sharing this with each other. During the intervision you are tapping into plenty of new levels. Sharing this with each other too early can lead to loss of direction.

- Place some extra chairs in the room. Let each participant decide who or what is sitting on that extra chair. This can be someone who was previously a member of the intervision group. It can also be a certain quality, an organisation or a moment in the future when… Every now and then someone can take his or her place on one of those chairs and thus become a representative of the person or the thing represented by the chair.

Points of focus

- It is important that everyone present is aware of what belongs and what does not belong to the intervision and why. There are dozens of systems present. With which systems does everyone want to work? How can your personal boundaries within those systems be indicated?

- Each judgement passed about each other, others and systems has an excluding effect. It divides. Your systemic wisdom can be found once you accept what is there. Sometimes it is enough to observe something's presence. Systemic intervision is a method that is weakened by division. It is normal for people to have their own opinions, but one must continuously wonder if it is strengthening to share this opinion (for which larger whole is it strengthening? For which larger whole is it not?).

Appendix

A

A.1 About Leanne Steeghs

Leanne Steeghs is a certified trainer and coach, organisational and family constellation facilitator and trainer at Trainers Academie and School voor Coaching. She integrates systemic methods, questions, interventions and constellations in leadership and team development programs, often in commercial organisations. After completing the master programme Organisational Constellations she decided that it was time to pass on her systemic wisdom through this book.

Acknowledgements

It feels right, for now, this is it. This book is ready to enter the world. I can let it go.

When I look out of the window I sense how my perspective has changed. Zooming out happens automatically. The summer beckons. Grateful words find me, there is no need to think about them.

Nell and Karin: you were my gateway to this work. Thank you for the clear explanations, they triggered my curiosity.

Morten: you are my example and mentor when it comes to exciting themes. You taught me to never avoid anything. Thank you for that.

Wibe: thank you for sharing your traditional knowledge about the body's signals; it sharpened my observations.

Jan Jacob: thank you for your generosity and encouragement to take this work a step further, also in a commercial sense.

V8 women: you are my base. Thank you for your deep-rooted faith in me as a constellation facilitator.

Marcel: thank you for your unfailing love and the many cups of tea during the writing process.

Siets: you have enriched and inspired me with your own wisdom in this work. I am grateful that I met you.

A.2 About Siets Bakker

Siets Bakker has used her systemic wisdom in countless organisations in her role as an organisation consultant. She teaches directors, advisors and HR managers in public organisations how to put systemic aspects into practice in their policies and implementation. She trains colleagues in systemic work and is one of the first people to have brought systemic work from constellations to the workplace.

Acknowledgements

Everything went quiet. Where previously the words had been tumbling over each other in their rush to appear on my screen there was now a deafening silence. I suddenly realised how much I have that I am extremely grateful for; how many people over the course of fifteen years have deliberately, accidently or coincidently – by being in the right place at the right time – contributed to me writing this acknowledgement right now. What happens when I mention someone? What happens when I don't?

The only way to do this is by letting my fingers find the keyboard and discover what comes up on the screen...

Leanne, thank you for wanting to be my mirror and conscience with this book.

Kees, thank you for always being there for me.

Bas, thank you for being my friend.

Bouke, Lidwien, Marieke, Jan Jacob, Bert and everyone else, thank you for sharing your wisdom.

A.3 Sources for further reading

Bakker, S. *Handleiding systemisch werken*. Self-published, 2013.

Bryan, B., Goodman, M. and Schaveling, J. *Systeemdenken, ontdekken van organisatiepatronen*. The Hague: Academic Service, 2006.

Delft, F. van. *Overdracht en tegenoverdracht*. (5th press) The Hague: Boom Lemma, 2012.

Hellinger, B. *Succes in werken en leven*. (4th press) Avenhorn: Het Noorderlicht, 2014.

Hellinger, B. *De kunst van het helpen*. Avenhorn: Het Noorderlicht, 2012.

Hendriksen, J. en Brasser, A. *Individuele opstellingen binnen coaching*. Amsterdam: Boom/Nelissen, 2013.

Herbig, R. *De adem – bron van ontspanning en vitaliteit*. (4th press) Haarlem: De Toorts, 2014.

Kaat, S. en Kroon, A. de. *Systemisch adviseren*. Avenhorn: Het Noorderlicht, 2013.

Stam, J.J. *Vleugels voor verandering*. Avenhorn: Het Noorderlicht, 2012.

Stam, J.J. *Het verbindende veld*. (3rd press) Avenhorn: Het Noorderlicht, 2009.

Thieck, en Zeeuw, B. van der. *Systemisch transitie management*. (2e druk) Amsterdam: Boom/Nelissen, 2014.

Varga von Kibéd, M. en Sparrer, I. *Ganz im Gegenteil, Tetralemmaarbeit und andere Grundformen Systemischer Strukturaufstellungen*. Carl-Auer-Systeme Verlag, 2014.

Veenbaas, W. en Goudswaard, J. *Vonken van verlangen*. (2nd press) Utrecht: Phoenix Opleidingen, 2005.

Veenbaas, W. en Goudswaard, J. en Verschuren, H.A. *De Maskermaker*. (2nd press) Utrecht: Phoenix Oplei- dingen, 2008.

Veenbaas, W. en Weisfelt, P. Persoonlijk leiderschap. (4e druk) Amsterdam: Boom/Nelissen, 2011.

Veenbaas, W., Baardspul-Schipper, I., Reinalda, S. en Broekhuizen, M. *Passe-partout*. Utrecht: Phoenix Opleidingen, 2007.

Wissen-van den Broek, L. *Naar eer en geweten*. Avenhorn: Het Noorderlicht 2016.

www.ingramcontent.com/pod-product-compliance
Lightning Source LLC
Chambersburg PA
CBHW051118200326
41518CB00016B/2544